on FIRE
at WORK

on FIRE
at WORK

HOW GREAT COMPANIES IGNITE PASSION IN
THEIR PEOPLE WITHOUT BURNING THEM OUT

ERIC CHESTER

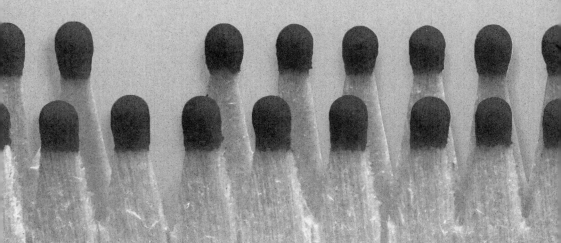

Sound Wisdom

P.O. Box 310

Shippensburg, PA 17257-0310

For more information on foreign distribution, call 717-530-2122.

Reach us on the Internet: www.soundwisdom.com.

ISBN 13 HC: 978-0-7684-0816-4

ISBN 13 Ebook: 978-0-7684-0817-1

Library of Congress Control Number: 2015954905

For Worldwide Distribution, Printed in the U.S.A.

5 6 7 8 / 19 18 17

on fire at work /ôn ˈfī(ə)r ˈat wərk/
▶ **adj. 1.** highly motivated to perform
2. feeling energized and joyful while on the job
3. extremely committed
4. determined to perform above expectations
5. the level beyond employee engagement
▶ **syn:** productive, loyal, all-in, inspired, dedicated
▶ **ant:** lazy, apathetic, careless, checked out,
inattentive, lackadaisical, halfhearted, dispassionate
(see also: **PROFITABLE COMPANY, EMPLOYER-OF-CHOICE**)

Firestarters

I owe a huge debt of gratitude to my editor and collaborator, Carolyn Daughters. Writing this book has been a daunting task that has challenged me to the core, and you've talked me off the ledge more than once, Carolyn. I owe you big time.

Thanks also to Blake Dvorak for helping to capture and refine my ideas and words and for providing important research along the way.

A shout-out to my friend and colleague of 30 years, Mark Sanborn, who always drops whatever he's working on to give me sage advice and guidance. Thanks for making my success your priority, compadre.

To Nido Qubein, who is a leader's leader. Nido, you set the standard of excellence for me in writing, speaking, and making a noticeable difference in the world. I am deeply honored that you would introduce me to your highly influential friends and business partners and then also agree to write the Foreword for this book. Wow. I am richly blessed.

To my coach, Dave McLurg. Dave, you are a brother and an inspiration, and you will always be the Chairman of my board.

To David Wildasin and his remarkable team from Sound Wisdom. I knew you were the right partner for this project from the moment we first talked. Your new-school approach to publishing will soon be the envy of all the old-school publishers in New York.

Finally, a monumental note of appreciation to the many remarkable business leaders who were interviewed for this book. No one is going to read these pages to hear what Eric Chester thinks; instead, they'll read the book so that they can tap into the wisdom and experience each of you brings on how to create a compelling, sustainable, on-fire workplace culture. Thank you for allowing me to peel back the curtains and share your ideas, practices, and strategies with the world.

Contents

Foreword

Here's the thing about culture: It transcends.

It transcends the products you sell, the services you render, and even the strength of your brand.

In *On Fire at Work,* my friend Eric Chester offers an insightful look at successful organizations that experience a bountiful cycle of enlightened self-interest.

Extraordinary companies want to provide outstanding service to their customers. Extraordinary employees want to work at an organization that fosters an impactful workplace culture. Customers love to experience extraordinary service from loyal and committed employees. Everyone wins.

As president of High Point University in High Point, North Carolina, I have a deep appreciation for the influence an effective culture can have when it is intentionally fostered. Having led this university through triple-digit growth in enrollment, fundraising, land acquisition, faculty positions, and more (during the great recession in the last ten years), I can tell you that our transformed culture made it possible.

When Eric informed me that he was working on this book, I was pleased, but not surprised. His research and publications on the subject have inspired me over the years and directed my own efforts to craft a culture that is distinctive, relevant, and valuable to the students and families who seek to enroll at High Point University (www.highpoint.edu).

Every organization has a culture. Some leaders cannot define it. But customers always can based on their experiences. They observe, feel, and talk about your organization—either positively or negatively. If you could hold a mirror up to your business, your culture would be the reflection.

In a world that forces everyone to compete on a global platform, not merely a continental stage, your organization faces stiff competition. That can be good. Contrary to the beliefs of many, you can no longer compete strictly with your strengths. Anyone out there can ship it as fast as you can, build it as strong as you can, and promote it as widely as you can. Your clients will only build a relationship with you if they value the experience you provide. And that experience is delivered on the strength or weakness of your company's culture.

Let me say it another way:

We compete on our differences, not our strengths. The experience you provide is your biggest differentiator. Your culture is what delivers the experience. So, culture transcends. It transcends every other aspect of your business.

An extraordinary culture is not what allows you to charge a premium price for your offerings; it's actually much bigger than that. An extraordinary culture is what makes your customer feel good about buying from you, regardless of the price. And then advocating you to the marketplace with conviction and on merit.

In this book you will find clear definitions, practical systems, and executable strategies to build, sustain, and enhance the culture of your organization. Eric's experience in the field coupled with his methodical delivery of content will give you a road map for cultural significance.

Sincerely,
NIDO R. QUBEIN
President, High Point University
nqubein@highpoint.edu

Chapter One

Steak Knives, the Old School, and the New Deal

"We're adding a little something to this month's sales contest. As you all know, first prize is a Cadillac El Dorado. Anybody wanna see second prize? Second prize is a set of steak knives. Third prize is... you're fired."

In the 1992 film *Glengarry Glen Ross*, Blake—famously portrayed by Alec Baldwin—issues this decree, exposing an artful display of insult and injury in the guise of a motivational speech to the troops. Called in on a "mission of mercy" for a beleaguered office of real estate salesmen, Blake unleashes a five-minute smackdown on the hapless bunch, something reminiscent of the abuse a battle-hardened drill sergeant might give boot camp recruits on their first day. There's so much contempt spewing from Blake's lips that it's easy to lose count of how many times he offends his targets with every slur under the sun. The salesmen can hardly believe their ears.

At first they think it's all a joke...until Blake tells them they're all fired. That's followed by the "happy" news that they've got one week to turn things around if they want to keep their jobs.

"Oh...have I got your attention now?" he asks sardonically.

It's not a joke, but it is amusing to watch—so long as you're not on the receiving end. No one, not the characters and certainly not the viewing audience, believes that Blake's "pep talk" will have any positive effect on employee morale. Indeed, it's not meant to. It's really a termination notice masquerading as a rally cry. The gist is that at least half of the office will lose their jobs. The sales contest exists simply to decide who's going to get the heave-ho. And if you're not in favor of the way you're being treated? Hit the road.

The film portrays a classic old-school environment fueled by fear—fear of being thrown into the dark abyss of unemployment at a moment's notice. Moreover, in this Machiavellian world your boss isn't your ally but rather your enemy, and he can push the button to the trapdoor you're standing on and ruin your life at any moment.

In this kind of culture, there are no winners. There are only survivors.

And those survivors are rewarded with steak knives. In this classic scene, steak knives are an insult, a booby prize no one really wants, a symbol of mediocrity. But getting them at least means you can keep your job. So there's some small redeeming value to them I suppose. (You get to keep your job, that is, until the next time Blake arrives on the scene. What'll happen then is anybody's guess.)

It's hard to believe that workplaces like the one depicted in *Glengarry Glen Ross* could still exist in 2015 and beyond, but some do. And while they're more plentiful than you might imagine, this book is not about terrible workplace cultures and despicable bosses.

In my research for this and other books, I've come across a vast number of organizations that, while nothing like the one described above, still operate under a winner-take-all ethos. Top performers get the El Dorado, struggling performers are terminated, and the vast majority sandwiched between those extremes are held at bay and ignored. This majority tends to feel as if they're in some kind of steak knives purgatory, and—no big surprise—their performance usually reflects the limbo in which they live. Their goal is to escape the axe, so they keep their heads down and fly beneath the radar. For them, employment heaven is a dream far off into the future when they find a better job at a better company.

A staff made up of Steak Knives. That's some employee pool.

There's no need to belabor the point that your success—and the success of your business—is tied directly to (1) the quality of the people you attract to your organization, (2) your proficiency in getting those people to consistently perform up to and even beyond their potential, and (3) your ability to keep them on your payroll for as long as possible.

And all of that hinges on one thing. Your culture.

Corporate Culture, Old-School Style

In the late '70s and early '80s, I worked my way through college as a grunt/gopher in a 50,000-square-foot freight salvage warehouse filled to the rafters with everything from 55-gallon drums of rubber cement to cornflakes to submarine batteries. This odd business was owned and managed by a tough-as-nails man who came of age during the Great Depression and whose perception of life was formed during that period as a homeless teenager and later as a soldier in World War II. That iron-fisted boss was also my father.

Dad's rugged path to owning his own business left him with zero sympathy for people who encountered unpleasant working conditions. The way he saw it, a job, any job, was a good thing. You worked to live and you lived to work, and when the man who signed your check told you to jump, the only acceptable response was, "How high, sir?" Dad didn't understand the word "quit" and would never allow his only son to utter it in any context, especially not when it came to work. You cannot fathom some of the tasks he charged me with during my tenure as his "apprentice."

My father was, in a term, Old School. We'll be referring to the Old School a lot throughout this book as a catchall phrase that defines those workplace cultures that operate from a command-and-control, top-down, "my way or the highway" mindset. However, don't think that you have to visit the Smithsonian to see an Old School culture on display. The Old School outlook isn't reserved for a particular age group or demographic. It's not a peculiar tenet of certain industries or professions. You can find it alive and well in the most progressive, arcade game-filled, relaxation lounge-laden tech startup in Seattle. Likewise, you can find the exact opposite in the most mundane, cubicle-regimented accounting firm in Birmingham. This way of thinking transcends the generations and is still very much in play at companies across the globe.

In fact, there's a good chance that your own experience includes working in an Old School culture or reporting to one or more bosses who embodied Old School ideals. What they demanded of you as an employee—and what you wanted from them as an employer— were directly at odds. The credo woven into that culture was one best summarized by Blake in *Glengarry Glen Ross*: "If you don't like it, leave."

Much of the Old School mentality is based on a perception that labor and management are at constant odds. Workers aren't "motivated"; they're coerced and prodded. Workers aren't passionate; they're lazy and insolent. Fear keeps workers in line, not a shared commitment to the success of the company. This friction between boss and employee assumes the interests of both groups are in direct opposition, so each must constantly battle the other to get what they want, all the while working "together" to survive (employee) and keep the company alive (employer).

If all this sounds slightly melodramatic, it's because I want to make the basic point that the Old School feels outdated today. But that doesn't mean it's extinct. Champions of the Old School can point proudly to highly successful corporations and industries that have been pragmatically built in accordance with this very approach. If it worked then, shouldn't it work now?

The Old School Deal

Today's Old School employers don't place much credence in buzzword-sounding mumbo jumbo like *employee engagement* and *workplace culture*. For the most part, they're fair-minded, practical people who pay wages in exchange for labor. So if you want one of their paychecks, dammit, just do what's asked of you and keep your mouth shut. That's "the deal" as they see it.

What's inherent in the Old School mindset is the assumption that the exchange of money for time and effort is sufficient. In other words, the financial deal that exists between an employer and an employee—compensation for work performed—is the *only* thing that really matters. You took the job knowing what you were going to have to do and how much you'd be paid to do it, so keep your head down and your nose to the grindstone.

Motivation? "The economy's shaky, and there are a lot of unemployed people out there who would gladly take your job (and could probably do it a lot better), so get busy."

Recognition? "If your name is spelled correctly on your paycheck, you've been recognized."

Advancement? "You're lucky to have this job, so stop fantasizing about the one you don't have."

When jobs are scarce or the wage offered is above market rates, workers will grudgingly accept "the deal" and do what's asked of them for fear of getting kicked to the curb. On the other end of the spectrum, when the economy improves and jobs are plentiful—or when the wage offered is nothing to write home about—Old School employers struggle mightily to attract and retain highly skilled people, and it's nearly impossible for those employers to keep the Steak Knife masses performing at an optimum level.

This may be why many Old Schoolers see today's workers as soft, spoiled, and lazy. These leaders don't get why a decent wage and fear of job loss aren't enough to motivate workers to step up and do what needs to be done. What's fair is fair. After all, they themselves came up through the Old School and paid their dues, and now it's time for these young upstarts to pay theirs.

Unhappy Employees Are Unproductive Employees

As my friend and best-selling author Dan Pink so aptly puts it, "Stories are good; data is better." A little data goes a long way, however, so let's hone in on a few representative (and very telling) statistics related to culture and employee engagement.

Gallup's 2013 "State of the American Workplace" poll surveyed 350,000 employees over a three-year period, and the results couldn't have been clearer: A vast majority of American workers—70 percent—are not engaged in their jobs. Then the kicker: "Gallup estimates that these actively disengaged employees cost the U.S. between $450 billion to $550 billion each year in lost productivity. [These employees] are more likely to steal from their companies, negatively influence their coworkers, miss workdays, and drive customers away."[1]

According to an even newer study from Deloitte titled *Global Human Capital Trends 2015: Leading in the New World of Work,* lack of employee engagement is the top issue currently facing a whopping 87 percent of HR and business leaders, up from an already startling 79 percent last year. The February 2015 survey of more than 3,300 HR and business leaders in 106 countries also revealed the following:

> The number of HR and business leaders who cited
> engagement as being "very important" doubled from
> 26 percent last year to 50 percent this year.

> Some 60 percent of HR and business leaders surveyed said they do not have an adequate program to measure and improve engagement.

> Only 12 percent say they actually have a program in place to define and build a strong culture.

> A mere 7 percent of those surveyed rated themselves as excellent at measuring, driving, and improving engagement and retention.[2]

While alarming, these statistics aren't news to most executives and managers. Every day leaders struggle with the multitude of problems that come with a disengaged workforce. And when they seek solutions, they find unsatisfactory answers. Pay them more. Offer a dental plan. Be more like Google.

Numerous studies have shown that better compensation is an ineffective motivator, as is offering a tableau of "bennies" like 401(k), health insurance, and two-week vacations. As for Google (or the dozen other companies usually cited as exemplars of workplace engagement), the reality is that most businesses aren't flush with Google's cash, nor do they have the luxury of handpicking employees from among the top applicants in the world.

There's an incredible amount of research out there, but let's not get lost in the numbers. Instead, let's just use uncommon common sense. Regardless of which study you point to, there's little question that an overwhelming percentage of people aren't happy at work. They don't like their jobs or the company they work for. They can't envision the way up and out of the hole they're in. Some of them are perpetual jobseekers, always on the prowl for the next best thing. And even if they haven't yet started hunting for a new job, they probably could stand to amp up their performance and productivity. One thing's for sure: This disengaged bunch is not your dream workforce. Not by a long shot.

Engagements Don't Last Forever

Roy and Beth have been dating for a year. One night after a romantic dinner in a posh restaurant, Roy pretends to drop a napkin on the floor. While reaching down to get it, he falls to one knee, pulls a big, shiny ring out of his coat pocket, and proposes to Beth. Totally caught off guard and beaming with joy, Beth tearfully accepts.

The two are now engaged.

Six months later, Roy and Beth's engagement comes to a screeching halt.

What happened?

They got married. The engagement ended the moment the marriage began.

The moral of this story? Don't sweep people off their feet with a sexy job posting, romance them throughout the interview process, and propose to them with a pie-in-the-sky commitment to a rosy future only to kiss engagement goodbye the day they begin their new jobs.

Engagement is a two-way street. It won't work if only one of the parties is engaged. That means you (the employer in this scenario) can't get the engagement you desire without also giving engagement in return. And, as will soon become clear, it's in your best interests to be the first to the altar.

Many if not most employees arrive to the job on day one fully engaged, which is to say they have a vested interest in meeting or even exceeding your expectations. Like you, they're optimistic about the opportunities of the job, and like you they want to put their best face forward and make a strong first impression to gain your trust and be perceived as a great fit with promising long-term prospects.

The challenge facing employers isn't how to engage employees. It's how to keep the fires of passion burning once the honeymoon period is over.

It's Not the Birds and the Bees, but the ERs and the EEs

Every employer wants employees who possess the skills needed to get the job done. Employers can either hire people who arrive on day one with those skills or hire people with the intent to train them. These days, having the most highly skilled workforce isn't necessarily enough to bring about the desired results.

In doing research for my one of my previous books, *Reviving Work Ethic: A Leader's Guide to Ending Entitlement and Restoring Pride in the Emerging Workforce* (Greenleaf 2012), I asked more than 1,500 business owners, leaders, and managers across myriad organizations and industries what they truly wanted from their employees. While today's employers want a highly skilled workforce, the findings revealed that what employers prize even more are employees who possess—and who consistently demonstrate—seven core attributes:

> **positive attitude**—be happy, cheerful, upbeat, optimistic people with a "can do" spirit

> **reliability**—be dependable, punctual, "no excuse" performers

> **professionalism**—dress, groom, and conduct themselves to best represent the company

> **initiative**—always try to learn, improve, and do whatever is necessary to add value

> **respect**—follow company policies and show respect for authority and the chain of command

> **integrity**—be honest, ethical, truthful, and forthright in all situations

> **gratitude**—go above and beyond expectations to deliver outstanding service to all

The seven attributes listed above are often referred to as *soft skills*. These soft-skill attributes are the non-negotiable character traits employers demand from every employee, so we'll call this the **ER List**.

In a perfect world, employers would hire from a deep pool of candidates who possess both the hard skills needed for the job and the ER List core values. Unfortunately, however, that particular pool of talent is shrinking (and getting more shallow each day), forcing employers to make more and more exceptions. No surprise there. What is surprising is where and how employers compromise—and to what degree.

Given a choice between a highly skilled worker with a marginal work ethic and a far less skilled worker with a solid work ethic, the latter will exceed expectations in the job almost every time. The truth is, I've yet to meet the employer who would purposely choose the worker with high skills and a marginal work ethic.

"We hire friendly and train skills," J.W. "Bill" Marriott told me when I asked him what made his 4,000-plus hotels a frequent honoree on *Fortune Magazine's* annual list of the 100 Best Places to Work.

If you want each and every employee in your organization to have the core values on the ER List, then it's only fair to reverse the question. What does every employEE want? More specifically, *what do your EEs want from you?*

The EE List: What THEY Want from YOU

It goes without saying that employees come to the workplace with needs and expectations that are as unique as they are. Nonetheless, if those employees were asked to make a list of seven things they expect from you, their employer, the list would probably look something like this:

- **compensation**—money, perks, benefits, and work/life balance

- **alignment**—meaningful work at a company with values that mirror their own

- **atmosphere**—a workplace that provides a safe, upbeat, enjoyable experience

- **growth**—opportunities to learn new skills and advance in their careers

- **acknowledgement**—feeling appreciated, rewarded, and sometimes even celebrated

- **autonomy**—encouragement to think and act independently and make decisions

- **communication**—being informed about relevant company issues and knowing the company is actively listening to their ideas and wants honest feedback

Let's go one step further and call these seven things the **pillars** of workplace culture—pillars, as in the seven side-by-side monuments that reflect the true identity of the company and the workplace community you've worked so hard to build.

The acid test to determine the validity of the employee demands on the EE List is quite simply a role reversal. Imagine that you've lost your job and you find yourself looking for work. A friend tells you that you have the perfect skill set for an opening at their company and that they can get you an interview for a position that's nearly identical to the one you just vacated. It sounds too good to be true, but,

> *The challenge facing employers isn't how to engage employees. It's how to keep the fires of passion burning once the honeymoon period is over.*

filled with optimism, you begin to prepare for the interview. Along the way, you discover that the position hits six of the pillars but is deficient on the seventh.

Let's say, for example, that the salary is less than half of what you were making before and not enough to sustain your current lifestyle without drastic changes. Or say the salary is terrific but you discover this company has been repeatedly fined for pouring toxic chemicals into your town's water supply. Or say that the company pays well and is very ethical, but reviews on Glassdoor.com indicate that an overwhelming number of employees claim they are micromanaged and forced to submit minute-by-minute personal productivity reports to their supervisor every day.

Which items on the EE List—which of these pillars—would you be willing to sacrifice? Naturally, if you were desperate for a job you'd be more willing to compromise here and there. But assuming your skills are in high demand and your options are plentiful, are there any items that you'd scratch off the list?

Of course not. The EE List includes those items that every employee, regardless of level or position or company or industry, wants and even expects in a job.

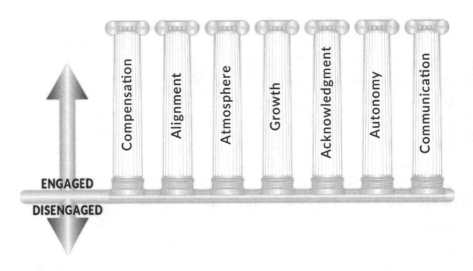

Assuming we're in agreement on what both parties are looking for in virtually any kind of employment relationship, we can then view these lists and see where "engagement" comes into play.

Engagement occurs when the basic needs and expectations of both the ER and the EEs are met. To put it another way, engagement occurs when an employer meets an employee's minimum requirements for compensation, alignment, atmosphere, growth, acknowledgement, autonomy, and communication. Engagement usually starts on day one of employment. Employees accepted the job in the first place under the assumption that their employer will meet whatever they see as their minimum requirements. This engagement continues until such time as employees feel frustrated in their attempts to actually get the things they expected. Said another way, engagement can last for a day, a week, a month, a year, or many years. Consistently meet the employees' minimum requirements, and the odds are good that you'll be consistently rewarded with engagement.

Broken Engagements

We began by talking about a workplace where most workers—the Steak Knives—fall in between the cracks and are left feeling marginalized and forgotten. Some of these people are engaged. Many of them aren't. This Steak Knife culture was the norm under the Old School regime, but it's rapidly becoming a dinosaur model for employers who, at minimum, desire engagement.

Those employers who see engagement as the end-all and be-all probably feel frustrated when their employees don't live up to those seven core values. Employees also feel let down when their employer doesn't hold up their end of the bargain. In either case, what results is a broken engagement—one or both parties disengage.

For example, say an employer feels that an employee overcommits and underdelivers, or perhaps workplace morale wanes when that employee is around. The employer begins to disengage from the employee. Engagement deteriorates into disenfranchisement when either or both parties feel that one or more of the expectations on their list aren't being honored.

Likewise, maybe an employee feels the employer doesn't offer as many opportunities for advancement as initially promised. Or perhaps the employee finds out that the company doesn't really practice what it preaches or that the computers they're issued are so closely monitored that every keystroke they make and all the websites they visit are recorded and scrutinized. What happens then? If your people don't get what they want, they start to disengage. Eventually they'll resign. Or, worse yet, maybe they'll stick around.

But here's the thing: Engagement isn't the ultimate goal—it's merely the starting point.

Beyond Engagement = On Fire

For many employers, employee engagement is the ultimate goal. Those employers should be careful what they wish for. To be fair, engagement is light years better than disengagement; however, the truth is that the engagement bar is still too low. Why not aim even higher? Are your employees flashing that shiny engagement ring? Are they singing your company's praises from the rooftops? Are they present and doing their jobs (no small thing), or are they all in (a monumentally big thing)?

Amazing things happen when either party in an ER/EE relationship begins to exceed the expectations set for them. For example, say an employee's exceptional performance allows her to advance faster than she anticipated. Or an employee's idea for adding a new product or service is approved and upper management recognizes him for this unexpected contribution in front of his peers. Or an entry-level technician takes it upon himself to learn how to repair a crucial piece of machinery that frequently breaks down, costing the company a boatload in downtime and maintenance bills; as a result, his manager gives him the freedom to take on additional projects that interest him. Or that sales rep who, without prompting, comes in on her day off to help the warehouse staff rebuild the conveyer system to get shipments out faster. Her manager gave her some time off the following week to thank her.

What often results is more than simple engagement—it's an ongoing cycle of *on-fire* commitment to the job, to fellow employees, and to the company. When employees are *on fire*, their energy level increases, sparking a similar increase in productivity, motivation, creativity, and performance. And when the people who work for you are *on fire*, the thought of looking for other employment isn't likely to cross their minds. Instead, they're going to want to stick around a little longer, and you're going to want to reward, promote, and invest more in them. We might call this the on-fire cycle.

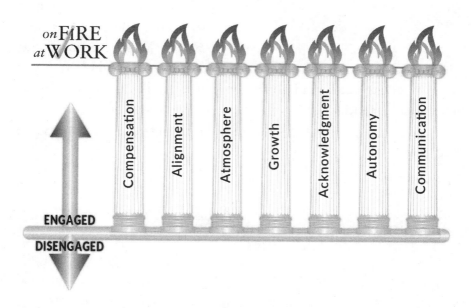

You Can Control Only What's Within Your Control

In your perfect world, you would want all of the people on your payroll to be as on fire for your company as you are. That's the dream of every ER (or at least it should be). But the reality is you can't force people to adopt an *on-fire* attitude. Likewise, you can't force anyone who works for you (or reports to you) to be positive, reliable, professional, or honest.

Like all successful relationships, an on-fire ER-EE relationship requires commitment, focus, and hard work. And that commitment, focus, and hard work begin with you.

Why begin with you? Why not begin with them? Because *you can control what happens on your side of the ledger.* Naturally, the owner or top executive in an organization has greater control over the seven pillars than a mid-level manager, and a mid-level manager has greater control over these pillars than, say, a shift supervisor. To whatever degree your authority reaches, *begin with you.* Make improvements where you can, and make those improvements early and often. If you want to create a legion of on-fire employees, making these improvements isn't negotiable. It's something you absolutely must do.

Here's the thing: Engagement isn't the ultimate goal—it's merely the starting point.

What follows in the chapters ahead is a field guide to help you do just that.

Employer-Employee Relationships That Bring Real Results

In this new economy, the cheese has already moved. Word has spread that a growing number of companies really take care of their people and have forged brand-new agreements that are getting better and better. And that's great news for the highly talented and technically skilled. The new deals being struck leave Old School cultures in the dust, forcing them to recruit leftovers from the employment marketplace scrap heap.

If you want to see these employer-employee deals in action, simply head west to Silicon Valley, home of Facebook, Google, Apple, HP, Netflix, eBay, Adobe, and countless others. These mega-wealthy powerhouses are deeply entrenched in a brutal war with each other for top talent, with no end in sight. This is a war none of them can afford to lose, and each is doing everything they can to make their deal just a little better than the others. The elements of each of these agreements differ, but what they have in common is that they're all rooted in a whole lot more than high salaries, flex schedules, casual Fridays, and free childcare. These aren't short-term "perk here, perk there" benefit packages intended to coax employees to stay somewhere in the ballpark of engaged for just a little longer.

In his recent book *The Alliance*, Reid Hoffman, founder of LinkedIn, says there's a fundamental disconnect in modern employment where employers ask employees to commit to the company without committing to those employees in return. Neither party trusts the other, both parties tiptoe around, and mid-level managers are caught, well, in the middle. Hoffman goes on to define the structure of a relationship based on a framework where promises are made that both parties can keep.

This emerging employer-employee relationship, as Hoffman sees it, is one where the company invests in employees' market value and employees, in turn, go all in and invest in the company's success. Neither assumes that the present relationship is going to last 40-some-odd years. Instead, each party is determined to keep the other's best interests at heart until a designated departure date, a specific project has been completed, or some other mutually agreed upon deadline has occurred. At that point, both parties have a meeting of the minds and decide how to proceed. They may agree to a new timeline. Alternatively, they may mutually decide that this particular employment relationship has run its course, in which case the employee will help to recruit a replacement, and the employer will use his or her influence and network to help the employee plug in somewhere else.

By forming a mutually beneficial alliance rather than simply exchanging money for time, both the employer and the employee can invest more deeply in the relationship and take the risks necessary to pursue and achieve bigger payoffs.

This all may sound like a scene from a futuristic movie, but it's happening at LinkedIn and dozens of like-minded companies. And because it's so appealing to the people involved, the alliance concept is spreading quickly through companies and industries worldwide.

It doesn't stop there. Whereas the Old School methodology is based on the straightforward exchange of time for money, forward-thinking organizations are adopting smart strategies that achieve the bottom-line results they seek. That's why Netflix no longer requires employees to adhere to a regular schedule and instead permits them to have unlimited time off whenever they feel they need it. Not to be out-cultured, Richard Branson, founder of Virgin Airlines, decided that his company would no longer track vacation time at company offices in the U.S. and the U.K. "Flexible working has revolutionized how, where and when we all do our jobs," he wrote. "So, if working nine to five no longer applies, then why should there be strict annual leave (vacation) policies?"[3]

But wait. When you allow employees to come and go as they please, productivity goes straight to hell, doesn't it? Not according to the Society for Human Resource Management. They report that workers who have been granted the freedom to choose when they work tend to take the same amount of time off—or even less time off—than workers with traditional vacation and sick time.

My father is likely rolling over in his grave.

A How-To Guide to On-Fire Employee Performance

Before we begin a much bigger discussion about on-fire performance in the workplace, let's highlight some of the topics we'll cover. For starters, there's a chapter devoted to each of the seven pillars.

- **Compensation:** We'll start with this well-documented topic, challenging the conventional wisdom that higher pay equals a more motivated workforce and reinforcing the importance of rewarding actual performance.

- **Alignment:** We'll examine the importance of aligning your values and vision with those of your employees and review well-known real-world examples of dos and don'ts.

- **Atmosphere:** What does your organization do to make work feel less like work? We'll pinpoint ways to create environments where employees actually want to work.

- **Growth:** Do your employees feel like you understand their career goals? We'll reviews steps you can take to help them articulate and achieve those goals.

- **Acknowledgment:** Employees want to feel appreciated, and they demand recognition for their contribution to your profits. Acknowledgment trumps recognition in today's workplace.

- **Autonomy:** Why micromanage your employees and second-guess their every decision? Leaders who give employees freedom and opportunities to pursue their passions can reap the rewards in the form of on-fire employees.

- **Communication:** Giving your employees a voice in the direction of the organization helps them see your goals as their own. Transparency is key.

Throughout, we'll go straight to the source—top-tier leaders of the world's best places to work. Successful company founders, CEOs, and other inspirational leaders will share their stories, secrets, and practical real-world strategies on how to build, not an engaged workforce, but *a workforce that's on fire.*

The founders/CEOs interviewed include J.W. Bill Marriott, CEO of Marriott; Gregg Saretsky, CEO of Canada's WestJet; Helmuth Ludwig, CEO of Siemens Industrial; Melissa Reiff, President of The Container Store; Joe DePinto, President and CEO of 7-Eleven; and Jostein Solheim, CEO of Ben & Jerry's. But before you get the wrong idea, it's important to note that this book isn't just for executives at large corporations. The guiding principle is that executives and managers at *any organization in any industry*—from Fortune 500 companies to the mom-and-pop pizza parlor down the street—can learn how to bring out the very best in their employees.

For this reason, the book also includes interviews with leaders at lesser-known organizations renowned for their exceptional workplace cultures, such as Wegmans, Build-A-Bear, Firehouse Subs, Vynamic, Western Governors University, and The Nerdery. And we'll go off the traditional grid to hear from inspirational leaders like Frank DeAngelis, Principal of Columbine High School—the scene of one of the most horrific tragedies in U.S. history. Each of these stories reinforces ways leaders in any industry can align, motivate, engage, and retain employees after a stock-price plunge, a hostile takeover, or something less dramatic but no less dangerous like worker discontent and workplace malaise.

This go-to reference provides *actionable steps you can take right now* to improve your culture and build a workforce that achieves exceptional on-fire performance day in and day out. It's meant for C-level execs, corporate and government senior managers, HR professionals, small business owners, franchisees, supervisors, and managers in every industry and at every size company or organization. Maybe you manage a 500-person team in a high-tech space or supervise 5 people at a corner deli. Either way, you'll find new ideas you can implement straight away. There may be limitations to what you can do, but rather than fixating on them, think instead about what you can do. Regardless where you work, ask yourself this: How can I exceed my employees' expectations and get on-fire performance in return?

In short, the pillars of an on-fire workforce remain true no matter the organization, industry, or annual profit. It all comes down to *culture*: Are you trying to motivate people to achieve occasional results, or are you building a workplace culture that fosters excellence and inspires everyone from senior managers to frontline minimum-wage employees to work harder, perform better, and stick around longer?

Again, we're focusing on what they want, not on what you want, because *giving them what they want is within your control.*

A New Deal

Over the last couple of decades, the archaic Old School frame of mind has given way to a New Deal where the EEs and the ERs join forces in a healthy, mutually beneficial relationship. When the ERs continually strive to improve the things their EEs want/expect in a job, their EEs are more committed, give the best they have, perform much better, and are less likely to leave.

I'm reminded of a scene in the classic film *The Ten Commandments.* Moses (played by Charlton Heston) is appalled at the treatment of the enslaved Israelites who labor nonstop on the Pharaoh's great building projects. Moses tries to make the Egyptians understand that treating their workers better will lead to better performance. His suggestions fall on deaf ears until he's finally able to put his theory into practice. Afterward, the Egyptians are amazed at how much more progress a better fed, better treated workforce is able to achieve.

Are you trying to motivate people to achieve occasional results, or are you building a workplace culture that fosters excellence and inspires everyone from senior managers to frontline minimum-wage employees to work harder, perform better, and stick around longer?

The Customer Is No Longer Number One

When I was a student in a high-school business course, my teacher repeatedly made mention of the Old School axioms "the customer is number one" and "the customer is king!" He wanted us to know our place in the business food chain, and back in the seventies, eighties, and perhaps even the nineties, those axioms held true.

Today, great companies recognize that the employee is number one. When an organization's people are prioritized, appreciated, and looked after with the same great care and concern formerly reserved for the organization's best customers, then and only then will the organization's employees take truly great care of their customers. In other words, great cultures take care of their people, and those people provide the kind of performance, attention to detail, and customer service that grows the organization.

The time has arrived to ignite passion in your people and prevent them from burning out.

Let's start with the pillar that's most likely their top concern. Compensation.

Notes

1.   Gallup, State of the American Workplace, 2013, http://www.gallup
     .com/strategicconsulting/163007/state-american-workplace.aspx.

2.   Josh Bersin et al., "Global Human Capital Trends 2015," Deloitte,
     February 27, 2015, http://www2.deloitte.com/us/en/pages/human
     -capital/articles/introduction-human-capital-trends.html.

3.   Richard Branson, "Why We're Letting Virgin Staff Take as Much
     Holiday as They Want," September 23, 2014, http://www.virgin.com/
     richard-branson/why-were-letting-virgin-staff-take-as-much
     -holiday-as-they-want.

Chapter Two

COMPENSATION:
Counterbalancing This and That

If you were to win $10 million dollars in the lottery, would you quit your job?

That's one of the revealing questions Gallup asks in its annual Work and Education survey. The percentage of Americans saying they would indeed quit after receiving this windfall has ranged from 31 to 44 percent. That means that at any point in time at least a third of your workforce would walk away from their jobs if they didn't need their paycheck. Sobering thought, huh?

While money might not be the primary motivator for every person in your organization, I'm guessing it would be an important consideration for you if you were considering a new job or a career move.

The reality is, unless your last name is Gates, Buffett, or Walton, the amount of your paycheck matters. For this reason, compensation will be the first of the seven cultural pillars we'll explore. However, the way we'll approach this topic may leave you with more questions than answers. That's by design. You see, there's no one right way to compensate all employees. Your objective as a business owner or leader is to find the best way to compensate *your* employees. And while having the right compensation methodology in place for your people won't guarantee that they will be on fire for you, the wrong compensation package will almost certainly ensure that you won't get on-fire performance from them, at least for any length of time.

Maybe you have complete authority over your company's compensation system and can make sweeping changes to it with a stroke of the pen. Or maybe you're at the opposite end of that spectrum and have little or no voice in how the employees you manage are paid for their efforts. Either way, it's near impossible to discuss employee engagement, performance, motivation, and workplace culture without examining the crucial role that compensation plays.

Origins and Principles

The word *compensation* is derived from the 17th-century Latin word *compensat*, which translates to "weighing one thing against another" or "counterbalancing." This counterbalance is the foundation from which all compensation programs and strategies arise; as such, it's crucial to remember what's at stake for both parties in this equation.

A business needs people to perform certain tasks in order to generate a profit.

An employee needs money in order to live and agrees to perform certain tasks in exchange for that money.

Both the business and the employee seek to counterbalance what they must give in order to get what they need or want, and it's to each party's advantage to give as little as possible in exchange for as much as possible. Both entities want to "win" in this compensation exchange and are primarily motivated by their own interests.

You can't blame the owners of a business for wanting to maximize their profits by getting the most out of every labor dollar they spend. Similarly, you can't blame employees for wanting to get every dollar they can for the time and labor they give their employer.

However, these basics increase in complexity when we layer in the vast array of emotions that invariably come into play, including—but not limited to—generosity, consideration, goodwill, appreciation, pride, greed, laziness, determination, respect, motivation, and…well, you get the idea. Factor those unknowns into any given employment relationship where both parties are, by nature, wired to want to get as much as they can by giving as little as possible, and things get interesting. To say the least.

The study of compensation as a cultural pillar is broader and deeper than merely calculating how much a business should pay its employees. Instead, we need to examine the delicate counterbalance of what each party in an employment relationship must bring to the table in exchange for what each party takes away. And to make the situation even more complicated, compensation is no longer bound by the traditional rules of trading dollars for an employee's production, sales, or time.

What's the Going Rate for a Happy, Engaged Employee?

"At the risk of offending some of our friends in the compensation profession, most pay systems suck a big egg," write Bill Catlette and Richard Hadden in their popular book *Contented Cows Give Better Milk*. "[Those pay systems] are not only broken, they make no sense. They not only fail to incent people to do their best, but in many cases, [they] actually induce them to do a poor job."[1]

A 2011 Gallup survey couldn't have been blunter: "There are no significant differences in employee engagement by income level." Indeed, Gallup divided employees into three income levels: those making less than $36,000, those making between $36,000 and $89,999 per year, and those making $90,000 or more. Engagement levels were the same at all three income levels. Roughly 30 percent of employees were engaged, while the rest were not engaged or were actively disengaged.[2]

Further, a 2010 study in the *Journal of Vocational Behavior* reviewed 120 years of research to synthesize the findings of 92 quantitative studies. The conclusions also couldn't have been any clearer: "[T]hose who make more money are little more satisfied than those who make considerably less. Moreover, relatively well paid samples of individuals are only trivially more satisfied than relatively poorly paid samples. For example, in 2009 dollars, a sample of lawyers earning an average of $148,000 per year were less job satisfied than a sample of child care workers earning $23,500 per year."[3]

Findings like these seem startling. At the same time, they make a simple point: An employee's paycheck and his or her level of engagement are not joined at the hip.

> An employee's paycheck and his or her level of engagement are not joined at the hip.

In other words, an employer shouldn't expect a compensation strategy to be the magic key that unlocks engagement. Having one of the prized compensation models or packages in your industry and/or your geographic area does two things for your business: (1) It helps you attract good people who are in demand, and (2) it decreases the likelihood that those good people will leave for a better offer elsewhere. It's the baseline from which on-fire performance begins.

Yes, Money Matters. But to What Extent?

There exists much confusion about compensation as the end-all and be-all of employee satisfaction (or, on the flip side, discontent). Deloitte, Gallup, the Society for Human Resource Management (SHRM), and data from numerous other polling and survey concerns indicate that pay increases are a key (or even *the* key) to employee engagement and retention. It's estimated that up to 80 percent of employees who voluntarily left their companies took a higher paying position with another company. There's little doubt that money matters to most everyone. The real question is, does it matter so much that it completely overshadows all else? Here, the data can be misleading.

Money is a simple, tangible metric to calculate, chart, and quantify. When asked a specific question regarding salary on a survey, respondents have little difficulty visualizing a higher salary and fantasizing about how they would live differently if they were being paid that amount. It's much more difficult for respondents to assign a value to more amorphous cultural factors like opportunity, recognition and rewards, workplace atmosphere, and personal autonomy. As a result, money is the survey item most commonly cited as a top concern.

As a landmark study published in *Psychological Science in the Public Interest* reveals, pure economic metrics (such as per capita income and compensation) fail to appropriately measure the happiness of a given society. In the article, authors Edward Diener and Martin Seligman argue that certain "well-being indicators" are a better metric for happiness. Said another way, a wealthy country is not necessarily a happy country. While the study focuses largely on macro-economic issues, it also delves into happiness at the organizational level, which is where it becomes relevant to us. Without getting too deep in the weeds of this tricky issue, the authors conclude that beyond a certain point money stops providing happiness.[4]

The "diminishing returns" nature of money means that compensation is merely a *foundational* component of workplace happiness. At a certain point, money ceases to be a motivator. The time at which that point is reached depends on a variety of factors, not the least of which is the job itself, but what's clear is that it's reached fairly early on. And after an employee hits that point—when that employee's minimum expectation (money) is met—then money alone won't tend to motivate the employee to go above and beyond.

Ineffective Compensation Models, Practices, and Policies

The most commonly used compensation models tend to be Old School paradigms that do not lay the groundwork for *on-fire* employee performance. Before we explore some models that actually do ignite and sustain passion and performance, let's take a closer look at four models that don't work:

1. Promote the Idea That One Size Fits All

2. Exchange Money for Time

3. Race to the Bottom of the Wage Scale

4. Dangle Nebulous Carrots

Promote the Idea That One Size Fits All

If every business were exactly the same and every person in that business performed the exact same tasks in the exact same manner and achieved the exact same end results, it would only be fair to pay each employee the exact same wage. Of course, such a scenario is highly improbable if not impossible. Moreover, such a scenario assumes not only that the business seeks the same outcome from each and every person, but also that every person wants the same outcome from the business.

Employees produce various outcomes in various degrees at various times, and each has various needs and wants. While it would be far simpler for a business to pay all employees the exact same amount, it would be unfair to each of them—and it would also be unfair to the business. The following parable better illustrates this idea.

THE SAWMILL

Jake and Justin, 23-year-old twin brothers, worked at a large sawmill not far from where they grew up.

Even though both had essentially the same job title and duties, Justin was paid significantly more than Jake. Curious as to why, the father asked the sawmill's owner, a longtime friend of his, about the variance. In response, the owner invited his friend to drop by the mill and casually observe the work being done.

After the father showed up at the mill, the owner called Jake into his office and said to him, "There's a trucker at the gate with some logs he wants to sell. Bring me the details." Within fifteen minutes, Jake returned and said, "I checked out the load. It looks like he's carrying about 40 to 50 large logs, mostly pine, and all appear to be in pretty good shape." The owner thanked Jake and dismissed him from his office.

The owner then summoned Justin and made the same request. A half-hour later, Justin came back and said, "I counted 38 pines. Most are about 20 feet and are in really good condition. There are also 11 aspens that are slightly shorter, and all but 3 are in pristine condition. The trucker wants $1,000 for the whole load. Sam McHenry was down here last week looking for aspens for a large furniture project, so I called him and asked if he's still in the market for aspens. He told me he'd take the eight good aspens off our hands and offered $150 for each. If we accept his offer, we'll make all our money back plus 20 percent, and the 38 pines will be pure profit." The owner told Justin to sell the aspens to McHenry, then thanked him and sent him on his way.

The owner looked over at the father. "If this were your mill, would you pay those two employees the same amount?"

"Absolutely not," the father said. "It wouldn't be fair."

Your industry has its own set of rules, and your business is unique within that industry. Further, not every employee in your organization has the same experience, the same skills, or the same workplace responsibilities. One size doesn't fit all because it's impossible to rationalize paying all employees the same—at least not when your goal is to generate lasting, on-fire results from all the employees in your organization.

While your employees don't all deserve the same compensation, each employee does deserve to be compensated fairly. Fair compensation. That's the key.

Paycheck vs. Total Compensation

When asked about their compensation, most employees think only of their base pay plus any bonuses they expect to receive. However, part (maybe 10 percent or maybe even 50 percent or more) of their total compensation could come in other forms that reward them for their contribution to the organization. These other forms could include profit sharing, a retirement or a pension plan, sweat equity, and opportunity income (e.g., skills training, professional development, and tuition reimbursement).

That's why it's important to impress upon potential recruits—as well as existing employees—that their compensation goes well beyond their negotiated salary. Shine the light on "total compensation" so they can make a more accurate appraisal of what they're really getting. Doing so will enable them to better compare their total package against offers from other suitors.

Remember, base pay never tells the whole story.

Exchange Money for Time

While myriad compensation programs and methodologies are being used in the workplace today, most involve the exchange of time for money. These three are the most popular:

> hours/shifts worked x hourly/shift rate = gross pay

> weekly/monthly/annual salary = pre-negotiated contract amount

> job title and/or earned certification(s) + years of experience = salary/year

Each of these models is formulaic and straightforward, but unless you're paying the highest rates in your industry these models aren't going to set your organization apart from your competitors, at least not from an employee's perspective. Rather than experiment with such a crucial component of attracting, engaging, and retaining workers (and perhaps even agitating the gods of HR and legal compliance), many employers opt to use the pay rate system that's most common in their specific industry. That's because it's easier to deal with a straightforward math problem than with a more elaborate calculation that involves a thorough assessment of each employee's real, day-to-day value to the company—a calculation that differentiates between the Jakes (moderately engaged employees) and the Justins (on-fire employees) and compensates each accordingly.

While your employees don't all deserve the same compensation, each employee does deserve to be compensated fairly.

Studies show that engagement rises when employees are paid in direct proportion to their contribution to their company and/or the value they bring to their organization. Likewise, when time spent on the job is the primary metric for calculating paychecks, employees tend to focus on doing only that which is necessary to keep their jobs. Many compensation plans reward people based solely on the years of experience they have on the job. For example, all teachers with 5–10 years of experience make an annual salary that falls between X and Y, whereas those with more than 10 years of experience make between Y and Z. These kinds of plans only motivate young superstars to leave for careers where results are rewarded more than job tenure. And every organization I've worked with over the past 15 years is trying very hard to attract and retain young superstars.

Millennials, as a cohort, are growing increasingly resistant to the Old School practice of investing years in low-paying internships or entry-level grunt work as the gateway to a better-paying job. For them, time trumps money, and even though they value both, time away from work has replaced money as the key factor in many employment compensation negotiations.

Imagine calling in one of your younger employees for a review. You've been pleased with her performance, and you tell her she has earned a pay bump. But before you can tell her how much, she tells you that the best raise you can give her is to allow her to work fewer hours each week for the same pay she's currently receiving.

Your head would explode! This kind of request probably runs counter to everything your own work experience has taught you. After all, isn't the universal workplace goal to advance in one's career and earn a bigger paycheck?

Think about it. You'd never rush home and tell your spouse or significant other, *"Hey honey, I got a 10 percent raise today! It'll be the same amount on the paycheck, but from now on I can leave the office at 4:12 instead of 5:00."*

The thing is, many members of Generations X, Y, and Z do not value nor do they blindly accept the *"more money at all costs"* Old School mentality. Messages like *"keep your head down and your nose to the grindstone and someday this will all pay off"* tend not to work with them. Times have changed, and the value people now place on work/life integration has been radically transformed over the last twenty years, particularly among those in the Millennial demographic.

In preparation for a speech to a large group of restaurant franchisees, I visited several locations and interviewed several dozen of their frontline hourly associates. To determine what they thought about their compensation, I asked each person, "Do you feel as if you're being paid a fair wage?"

One of the responses came from Trevor, a 20-year-old part-time employee working his way through college as a sandwich maker and cashier. That response spoke volumes about his generation's perspective on hourly wages.

"Today, yes," Trevor said. "Today it's pretty chill [quiet and slow] around here, so it feels like I'm being paid fairly."

"Then tell me about a day when you feel you're not being paid fairly?" I asked him.

"A day when customers are lined up at the counter from the moment I punch in. I have to work my butt off to serve them, and then when we close for the night the cleanup takes forever."

This conversation reveals the disengagement chasm that has existed between employer and employee since someone first came up with the idea of exchanging dollars for hours. You see, Trevor's pay is based solely on the amount of time he's at work. When he doesn't have much to do, he feels satisfied with his wage. Conversely, whenever Trevor is content with his compensation, his employer suffers because traffic slows and sales decrease. Trevor's employer benefits most when a long line of customers streams in throughout the day. But whenever that happens, Trevor's workload increases while his wage remains the same, so he feels like he's getting the shaft.

Trevor's goals and his employer's goals couldn't be more at odds. And in both scenarios, there's one clear winner and one clear loser.

Exchanging money for time is easy to calculate, but without any additional incentives or performance bonuses these time-based compensation models will disengage and demotivate your people faster than you can say "train wreck."

Race to the Bottom of the Wage Scale

Operating on razor-thin margins causes many employers to keep an ever-vigilant eye on labor costs. Whenever revenues dip, they immediately shift into payroll-trimming mode, making cuts wherever and however they can. Payroll trimming may often be standard operating procedure for businesses that compete solely on price, but it makes it extremely difficult to attract and retain a high-quality workforce.

Exchanging money for time is easy to calculate, but without any additional incentives or performance bonuses these time-based compensation models will disengage and demotivate your people faster than you can say "train wreck."

As this chapter is being written, two states in the U.S. are raising their minimum wage. This hotly debated topic has many solid arguments on both sides of the aisle. But rather than focus on what the minimum wage should be, let's explore when it might make good financial sense for a business to pay the minimum and when it might not.

Let's say your business employs people who either have very little experience in the workplace or none at all. And let's say you have to train those people not only how to perform low-level tasks in your business but also how to take on responsibility (e.g., clock in, dress and groom themselves for their shift, follow directions, and find productive things to do when business is slow). In this case, paying the least amount legally possible may be a decent strategy. However, if your goal is to attract and develop people who are a cut above the fray, people who could easily find another job like the one you're offering for the same wage or more, then paying as low a wage as you can legally get away with will only ensure that your business perpetually remains on the profit-eating hire/fire treadmill.

You've probably heard the age-old axiom that "if you buy cheap, you'll buy twice." The same premise holds true for employers who insist on hiring only the cheapest labor for each position in their company. The money saved on payroll will be gobbled up by additional costs in training, employee mistakes and blunders, lost sales, poor customer service, and employee turnover.

Dangle Nebulous Carrots

Carson, the son of a friend of mine, is an MBA whose passion centers on business mergers and acquisitions. Two years ago, Carson accepted a position with an investment bank that offered him an embarrassingly low starting salary but promised that he'd be seeing some nice bonuses as the firm closed large deals. Determined to prove his worth, Carson has worked a minimum of 55 hours each week, received stellar performance reviews, and even managed to bring in and close several profitable deals for the firm. While Carson highly values the experience he has received, his compensation has remained way under market value, and he has received only a few small bonuses that aren't even close to those the partners suggested would augment his small base.

Frustrated, Carson has approached the firm's partners about this pay inequity on several occasions, and each time they have placated him with hints of a big payoff in the future. Carson is supporting his wife and young toddler and has asked for specifics so he can plan accordingly. But using ambiguity as their primary tool, the non-committal partners have instead chosen to stall Carson. What they don't know but will soon learn is that Carson has interviewed with several competing firms and is preparing to make his exit.

One might think that this practice of dangling a nebulous carrot in an attempt to attract talent and effect high performance at bottom dollar would be extinct in the new millennium, but it's still commonplace. Even the best-intentioned ambiguous promises have no place in the compensation strategy of a great culture.

Effective Compensation Models, Practices, and Policies

To reiterate what we've already established, simply paying high wages and offering elaborate benefits won't guarantee that your employees will be *on fire* for you or your company; however, offering a poor compensation package will almost certainly guarantee that you won't get the best from your people and that your turnover will be much higher than necessary. With that thought in mind, let's examine three of the essential elements of today's most effective compensation models:

1. Strive for Transparency

2. Pay People More Than You Have To

3. Tie Employee Income to Employee Outcome

Strive for Transparency

Have you ever worked for a company where all employee wages were frozen until further notice because sales did not meet projections? There's nothing particularly unusual about such a course of action—it's quite common actually. Where frozen-wage policies become divisive is when employees start pinching pennies only to discover that top-level executives are driving home in new BMWs.

In many organizations, salaries and wages are a taboo subject, and in some organizations discussing what you make with coworkers is grounds for termination. Shrouded in secrecy, these cultures operate under a blanket of "don't ask, don't tell" thinking. The idea that what employees don't know won't upset them may have worked a few decades ago, but it's no longer the case. Employees now look for and expect sensible and uniformly applied compensation practices.

"My employees know exactly what I make," said Chet Cadieux, CEO of QuikTrip, a 13,000-employee chain of convenience stores that has made *Fortune*'s Best Places to Work list 11 years running. Chet talked to me about how QuikTrip employees are never left in the dark about what he makes, which cuts down on the animosity that so often arises between management and labor.

"We're constantly communicating with our employees," Chet said. "If I stood up in front of them and said things were bad and pay would be frozen, they wouldn't like it, but I honestly think they'd understand." Part of that understanding can surely be attributed to the fact that they would know whether or not Chet was tightening his own belt.

> *"My employees know exactly what I make."*
> —CHET CADIEUX,
> CEO, QuikTrip

Honesty, openness, transparency—these are the very attributes many organizations overlook or even dismiss outright, as if shining a light on what managers, directors, VPs, and those in the C-suite earn will somehow spark rebellion. This mentality is Old School. The real rebellion, the quiet, seething kind that builds up over time, starts when employees are left in the dark, free to weave their own stories out of the bits and pieces of information that they're given or that they dig up on their own. The company might have the best of intentions by forgoing annual raises (maybe doing so prevented layoffs), but unless employees know the pain is shared across the enterprise, they will grumble to their coworkers. And discontent simply breeds more discontent.

Let It All Hang Out

Tokyo Joe's, a chain of 30-plus fast casual restaurants in Colorado, Arizona, and Texas, is all about compensation transparency. So much so, in fact, that dine-in customers will find on their tables a colorful chart showing the various rates of pay, perks, and benefits Tokyo Joe's employees make, from the part-time cashiers all the way to the general managers. This information serves not only to attract potential job applicants but also to provide clear information on career paths for existing employees.

Pay People More Than You Have To

A growing number of highly profitable companies spanning a wide range of industries attribute their sustained profitability and successes to the practice of paying some of the highest wages in their respective industries. Let's look at two shining examples.

The Container Store, headquartered in Coppell, Texas, has made *Fortune's* list of the 100 Best Places to Work in America in each of the past 16 years. They hire according to a simple philosophy: "One great person equals three good people." Company president and COO Melissa Reiff told me the company maintains that one well-trained, well-compensated employee can do just as much as three adequately trained, adequately compensated employees. In line with this philosophy, The Container Store pays full-time floor employees an average of about $50K per year, which is almost double that which many other national retailers pay their full-time people for the same jobs.

To be clear, the company doesn't throw money at their people; they invest in them. Each full-time salesperson at The Container Store receives 263 hours of training during their first year. Compare that to the industry average of less than nine hours of training per year for people in comparable positions. These 263 hours of training translate into a remarkable difference in the service and support customers have come to expect and appreciate, as reflected in the average 20 compounded average growth rate (CAGR) The Container Store has experienced since its first store opened in 1978.

Of course, The Container Store isn't quick to hire anyone who can fog a mirror, as is the apparent practice with so many other retailers. In fact, Melissa said that they hire only about 3 percent of all who apply. But once you're brought on as a part of their team, chances are you're going to stick around. The Container Store boasts a turnover rate of less than 10 percent—not bad for an industry that had a median turnover rate of 67 percent for part-time workers in 2012.[5]

As Melissa explained, the company's compensation philosophy is "win-win-win": "Employees win because they're getting paid up to twice as much. The company wins because it gets three times the productivity at two times the payroll cost. But most importantly, customers win with extraordinary service."

Even though The Container Store treats each employee relatively the same, it asks more of those employees than your average retailer. And raises are still based on individual performance. The old saying "with great power comes great responsibility" applies in this case. At The Container Store, great compensation comes with great responsibility. If the employees didn't live up to the company's expectations, then customer service would suffer, leading to a drop in sales. In short, the employees' salaries would cut too deeply into profits, making the employees too expensive to keep.

Employees First and Last

The Container Store proudly promotes their brand as an employee-first culture. They recently created an Employee First Fund to provide grants to employees experiencing unforeseen emergencies like major medical situations, catastrophic events, and other unplanned personal and financial challenges. Although funding of the initial project came through the company, the fund is now supported through contributions made by employees and other company stakeholders.

But because each Container Store employee does the work of three typical employees at other retail establishments, The Container Store is able to provide them with superb salaries that not only lead to fantastic customer service but also strengthen their commitment to their employer. And it's far easier to get consistent on-fire performance from someone who thinks of their job as a career than it is from someone who's thinking of their job as a temporary transitional position.

Another example of paying employees more than is required can be found at the manufacturing facility of Ben & Jerry's renowned line of premium dairy products in Waterbury, Vermont. Most everyone in the organization feels as though they are being paid fairly, and in this case, "fairly" means above average.

"We start entry-level employees in our production facility at a 'livable wage' that is determined by a third-party and adjusted by a third-party every year," Jostein Solheim, Ben & Jerry's CEO, told me. "This wage depends on the geographic location of the work being performed because it must take into account the cost of living in that area." At this writing, the minimum wage in Vermont (where this epic ice cream is produced) is $8.73, but Ben & Jerry's employees start out at a minimum of $16/hour.

For the record, $16/hour as a base-pay starting point is not an easy compensation strategy to maintain, but it is one of many things that sets Ben & Jerry's apart. Jostein explained it this way, "If you're earning between $300,000 and $500,000, you're in 'silly money land.' But if you're earning $25,000 to $40,000 a year, a few extra dollars here and there make a huge difference in terms of the lifestyle you're able to live."

And it's not just an attractive starting wage that keeps Ben & Jerry's ahead of the curve. "Throughout the recession, our employees' salaries went up 5 to 6 percent because the cost of living rose so dramatically," Jostein told me. "We were giving salary increases of 5 percent back in 2008 when everybody else was cutting salaries." And make no mistake, their employees are keenly aware of that fact. It's one reason Ben & Jerry's has extremely low turnover. (Another reason could be that all headquarters and manufacturing plant employees get to take home three pints of ice cream each day!)

Indeed, recent research from Towers Watson shows employees who believe they are paid fairly are 4.5 times as likely to be highly engaged employees compared with people who do not believe they are paid fairly.[6] (Again, compensation is not a magic bullet. It's the minimum requirement for getting good employees in the door and keeping them.)

Tie Employee Income to Employee Outcome

People will support what they help to create. This popular axiom has become almost cliché in management-training courses for one reason: It's impossible to refute.

So if we know that to be true, why shouldn't the results people create also support them?

When employees have a selfish interest in the outcomes they create for their employer, they rejoice when company profits are high. They also feel the pinch when times are tight. Compensating employees in this manner eliminates the train wreck money-for-time model discussed previously by aligning the motivations and goals of the ERs with those of the EEs.

Organizations that break free from the Old School compensation mindset are much more capable of creating the foundation of shared objectives that is a prerequisite to sustained on-fire performance. For this reason, we might do well to examine what some celebrated cultures have achieved using different compensation strategies.

Flying High for Their Employer

With more than 10,000 employees, Calgary-based WestJet airlines has been widely recognized as one of Canada's best places to work, claiming the top spot in Waterstone Human Capital's study of Canada's 10 Most Admired Corporate Cultures multiple times. WestJet was also ranked in Aon Hewitt's 50 Best Employers in Canada 2015, a ranking the company has held for many years. These are just two of many cultural awards WestJet has received since their inception in 1996.

I had the pleasure of interviewing Gregg Saretsky, WestJet's CEO. The first thing he told me? "At WestJet, we compete on culture."

To learn more about what that meant, I asked Gregg how compensation fit into the company's cultural identity. In particular, I asked him about WestJet's renowned compensation plan. He told me that 85 percent of employees participate in their Employee Share Purchase Plan, which allows them to purchase up to 20 percent of their gross salary in WestJet stock. That amount is then matched by the company.

"At WestJet there is a very strong alignment between the needs of the business and the needs of the people through our culture of ownership," Gregg said. "When employees are performing in the best interests of the company and business results are as strong as they have been over our 19-year existence, then the stock performs well. Through their ownership program, WestJetters [WestJet employees] get a nice reward."

"At WestJet, we compete on culture."
—GREGG SARETSKY,
CEO, WestJet

Note the difference between a stock ownership program and a typical year-end bonus. With an ownership program, there isn't a set amount that each employee stands to gain should the company perform well. An ownership program is continuous, meaning that the employee is engaged throughout the year rather than just in the last quarter. Investments have the potential to grow (and grow big), whereas cash rewards are one-time deals.

As Gregg said, "The employees' DNA and the DNA of the business are absolutely in alignment."

Obviously, not every organization is set up to be able to offer a stock plan or profit sharing or even a commission structure. But for any employer that wants to be able to proudly boast that they "compete on culture," it's imperative to look for creative ways to tie incomes to outcomes.

Empowering Managers to Incent Individuals on the Spot

Salespeople who work solely on commission are paid in direct relation to the results they achieve; thus, the best (most successful) salespeople are self-motivated. Similarly, bartenders and restaurant servers who work for tips are highly incentivized to bring their best to the job. That's all well and good, but how do you incent a plumber, an administrative assistant, a graphic designer, a factory worker, or an accountant? How do you incent a high performer who's part of an underperforming department or team?

"We look at the market and make sure we have fair and complete compensation packages for our team members," Helmuth Ludwig, CEO of Siemens Industry, told me. "Interestingly, beyond this, there has to be an incentive structure or better 'recognition structure.'"

While a compensation package can help to attract and retain employees, it often does little to recognize when they go the extra mile and perform far beyond expectations. So how do you get on-fire results? Helmuth told me about Siemens' *You Answered* program, which recognizes employees for good work with small monetary awards. These are not the typical bonuses that other companies dole out at the end of the year. Rather, Siemens hands out cash rewards of $50, $100, or $200 to employees who have gone "beyond the normal," as Helmuth calls it. Siemens managers are encouraged to provide these rewards on the spot whenever they see one of their employees go above and beyond. And if the specific action of an employee merits it, the cash amount can go as high as a thousand dollars or more.

"It's a simple but very powerful system," said Helmuth, who has been at Siemens since 1990. Rather than bestowing large-scale bonuses as an incentive to certain divisions or groups for hitting a pre-specified mark, the *You Answered* program singles out individuals for exceptional performance. So even if the rest of the division comes up short, an employee in that division can still be celebrated for exceeding expectations.

"There are always impromptu opportunities to recognize extraordinary work," noted Helmuth. "Our program doesn't limit recognition to any group; instead, it applies to absolutely everyone."

When all employees are eligible to receive individual recognition and monetary rewards even when the company (or their specific unit or team) is underperforming, everyone is driven to perform at their best and the superstars on the team don't become disenfranchised.

Further, when rewards are both impromptu and immediate, they help solidify and perpetuate the effort behind a desired outcome. And managers love having a tool that enables them to recognize the many positive contributions their people are making rather than always having to focus on reprimanding and correcting any negative attitudes and behaviors they witness.

How Pay-for-Performance Changed the Culture at 7-Eleven

Joe DePinto picked a challenging time to accept the job of CEO at 7-Eleven. The year was 2005, and the company, a venerable icon in the convenience store industry, had suffered some seriously tough times. It had gone through a Chapter 11 bankruptcy reorganization in the early 1990s and had a few years of net store decline in North America, leading up to Joe's taking on the reins of 7-Eleven, Inc. But where other executives might have seen a declining business, Joe saw an opportunity.

"7-Eleven was both an iconic brand and a diamond in the rough," said Joe, explaining his decision in 2005 to leave GameStop, where he was president. "Personally, I felt the company needed a culture change."

And so Joe set out to accomplish one of the most difficult tasks in the business world—fundamentally change an established (in this case, 78-year-old) corporate culture. But Joe wasn't deterred. "Being able to lead a culture change was something that was very interesting and exciting for me."

The culture Joe encountered when he joined 7-Eleven was very insular. "We were really turned inward," he told me, explaining that the company had lost touch with its franchisees, whom Joe saw as the future of the business. But changing the insularity of 7-Eleven required a complete cultural overhaul, starting at the top. He began by symbolically renaming corporate headquarters the "Store Support Center."

One of the first and most difficult missions Joe took on in those early years was to transform the performance evaluation process. Joe saw the process as a chance to instill in his management team the values of what he calls "servant leadership." Instead of simply judging managers on the company's financial performance, the company would evaluate each employee's individual performance plus their servant leadership skills, which in turn would determine his or her compensation—otherwise known as "pay for performance."

Joe knew it wouldn't be a popular move. At least not at first.

"We had to change from a culture of entitlement to a culture of performance," he explained. "There are a lot of companies out there that don't look at it this way. Those companies don't put in place programs and processes that say we're going to evaluate you on performance. We laid out the standards and were very clear about them. It's not just about getting financial results. It's about getting results by leading with the values of a servant leader."

Joe created the Servant Leadership Performance Assessment that would henceforth be used to rate all employees. A visual representation provided by 7-Eleven best explains this assessment process. The nine boxes in the graphic represent the nine possible ratings employees—from store managers to executives—can receive during their performance review. The nine-block exercise identifies both *what* is achieved and *how* it is achieved.

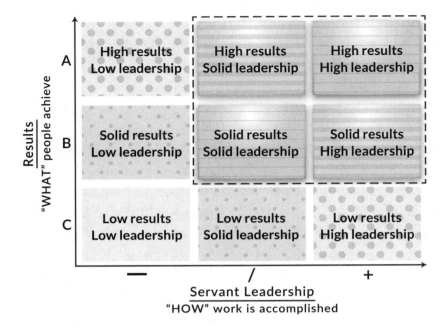

In the upper right-hand corner (striped boxes) are the top "servant leaders," those who achieve solid or high leadership (in accordance with the company's new cultural values) and solid or high results (exceptional performance).

The "development candidates" are those managers who have a mix of high, solid, and low leadership and results (dotted boxes). Instead of getting rid of these managers, the company saw their potential and chose to help them create and implement plans for improvement. Those in the lower left-hand quadrant (solid box) were employees who would likely leave the company because they had low results and low levels of leadership. This pay for performance plan initially caused some animosity from those ranked as middle of the road. Joe merely says, "It was a very difficult process." It wasn't a very fast one either. "It took five years to get it fully in place," he told me. "I'm really proud of it, but it took a long time to do."

It also worked, both culturally and financially. "If you look at our store numbers, you can see we have grown significantly as a company," Joe said. During his tenure, 7-Eleven went from opening a small number of stores in the U.S. and Canada to increasing the store count there by almost 2,500. 7-Eleven had slightly over 5,800 total stores across the U.S. and Canada at the end of 2005, and they have 8,300 stores today.

Earnings were just as impressive. In 2005 when Joe started, 7-Eleven had operating income close to $281 million. By the end of 2013, that number was around $518 million. The company's S&P credit rating improved from A to AA-, while its Moody's credit rating improved from Baa3 to Baa1. Joe also reached an important cultural milestone. During his tenure, 7-Eleven has increased the number of franchised stores in the United States from 66 percent to about 82 percent.

> "My idea was pretty simple: Provide top performers with huge growth opportunities, task them to help teach and train those in the middle, and manage out those who don't buy in."
> —JOE DEPINTO, CEO, 7-Eleven

And it all started by using compensation to affect culture. Said Joe, "My idea was pretty simple: Provide top performers with huge growth opportunities, task them to help teach and train those in the middle, and manage out those who don't buy in." What are you left with? Top performers whose pay is determined by their willingness and capability to exhibit the qualities of servant leadership and produce exceptional results.

Compensation Is Only the Baseline for On-Fire Performance

If your salary were doubled tomorrow, naturally you'd be thrilled, and you'd probably shift into a higher gear in an attempt to show your appreciation to your boss and your company. But how long would it take for the jubilant feeling to dissipate? How long before you would return to your pre-raise level of performance?

Now, imagine that your salary was cut in half tomorrow. How would your attitude toward your job change? How long would it be before your performance began to dip?

There's no question that compensation plays a significant role in how employees approach their jobs, how long they remain in their jobs, and how they feel about their employers. But as crucial as compensation is to a company's workplace culture, there's no evidence to suggest that it can ignite and sustain on-fire employee engagement. *It can, however, lay the foundation on which on-fire performance is built.*

 ## Igniters, Flamethrowers, and Burnout Extinguishers

To ensure you're using the best possible compensation strategy for your business, approach each of these questions first from the perspective of a leader in your organization and second from the perspective of an entry-level or mid-level employee. Answer the questions, then question the answers. See if the pay policies in your organization truly reward the actual value each employee brings.

1. **Recognize that fair pay means competitive pay.** How does your company's compensation package compare with that of your competitors? Do your people feel they are being paid fairly? Does your system put your employees on your side or pit them against you?

2. **Differentiate between the Jakes and the Justins.** What kind of strategy does your company have in place to identify employees who perform poorly vs. those who do good work vs. those who those who are on fire? In what ways is this strategy used to identify

employees who honor the company's values vs. those who do not?

3. **Compensate employees in accordance with the value they bring**. Does your compensation model reward employees according to their individual contribution? Does your strategy provide an incentive for people to consistently perform at their best?

4. **Fine-tune your compensation strategy**. In what ways can you strengthen your current compensation system to help you better reward star performers, provide training and support to develop underperforming employees who have potential, and weed out those employees who consistently underperform and fail to live up to your company's values?

5. **Pick a lane**. In the following scenario, which company is making the biggest mistake: The one that pays employees 15–20 percent more than they would make doing the same job for a nearby competitor, or the one that pays its employees 15–20 percent less than they would make if they worked for a competitor? Now, find someone who disagrees with you and debate the issue. Compensation isn't a magic key that unlocks engagement, but it does lay the foundation on which on-fire performance is built; thus, this thorny discussion is probably worth all the time and thought you're willing to give it.

6. **Incentivize your staff**. Consider the *You Answered* incentive program at Siemens. Are your managers able to reward their direct reports for doing outstanding work? If your answer is "yes," how much leeway do your managers have in doling out these incentives?

Are they able to give on-the-spot incentives without first obtaining approval from upper management?

7. **Increase your transparency.** In your opinion, does the transparency at QuikTrip make sense for your organization, or does it seem excessive? What kinds of problems could a company expect with this degree of transparency? Do your direct reports know how much you make? Should they?

8. **Help your people feel invested.** Consider how WestJet's stock ownership program creates loyalty and employee buy-in. How can you duplicate this degree of devotion in your company and make your employees feel like they are stakeholders in your organization's success?

9. **Reflect upon the times you've chosen to work for less than you could have:** Think of a time you volunteered to support a cause or consciously chose to work for less than your market value. What prompted this decision? Was the decision worthwhile for *you*?

10. **Assess the tools you most frequently use to incent your people.** Are you satisfied with the tools and systems you have in place? Are your employees satisfied with the wages they earn? How do you know?

Notes

1. Bill Catlette and Richard Hadden, *Contented Cows Give Better Milk: The Plain Truth about Employee Relations and Your Bottom Line*, (Contented Cow Partners, 2001), 168.

2. Nikki Blacksmith and Jim Harter, "Majority of American Workers Not Engaged in Their Jobs," Gallup, October 28, 2011, http://www.gallup.com/poll/150383/majority-american-workers-not-engaged-jobs.aspx. Tomas Chamorro Premuzic, "Does Money Really Affect Motivation? A Review of the Research," *Harvard Business Review*, April 10, 2013, http://blogs.hbr.org/2013/04/does-money-really-affect-motiv/.

3. Mark Savickas, *Journal of Vocational Behavior*, 2010, http://www.timothy-judge.com/Judge,%20Piccolo,%20Podsakoff,%20et%20al.%20(JVB%202010).pdf.

4. Ed Diener and Martin E.P. Seligman, "Beyond Money: Toward an Economy of Well-Being," *American Psychological Society*, 5:1, 2004, http://www.brookings.edu/Comm/events/20040603b.pdf.

5. "Hay Group Study Finds Employee Turnover in Retail Industry Is Slowly Increasing," Bloomberg, May 8, 2012, http://www.bloomberg.com/article/2012-05-08/aWdgOKjbTBXY.html.

6. Laurie Bienstock, "Using Compensation as a Springboard to Drive Employee Engagement," Towers Watson, 2011, http://www.worldatwork.org/adimComment?id=52476.

Chapter Three

ALIGNMENT: Inculcating Core Values from the C-Suite to the Custodian's Supply Room

At the end of the year 2000, a company based in Texas, its employees, and its stockholders had every reason to be optimistic. Forget optimistic—downright joyful. The company's market capitalization had increased from around $2 billion in the mid-1980s to roughly $70 billion. Its consolidated revenues were just over $100 billion, making it seventh on the Fortune 500. The company's stock price had increased 87 percent in 2000 alone.

But that wasn't all. Not by a long shot.

Named *Fortune Magazine's* "Most Innovative Company in America" for six years running, this organization received top marks for quality of management, quality of products and services, and employee talent. Their nearly 25,000 employees had the pleasure of knowing they earned a paycheck from one of *Fortune's* "100 Best Companies to Work For" for the past three years (in 2000 they ranked number 22).

Underlying all the success and accolades were the company's values. Communication. Respect. Integrity. Excellence. Those values were inscribed on office doors, shiny brass plaques, stock reports, and other corporate materials. They were plastered throughout the company's massive Houston headquarters, so much so that it was almost as if those values helped bolster the building's structural foundation. And they went further. They defined the values and tried to pinpoint what they really meant. Let's take a look.

> *Communication*: We have an obligation to communicate. Here, we take the time to talk with one another...and to listen. We believe that information is meant to move and that information moves people.

> *Respect*: We treat others as we would like to be treated ourselves. We do not tolerate abusive or disrespectful treatment.

> *Integrity*: We work with customers and prospects openly, honestly, and sincerely. When we say we will do something, we will do it; when we say we cannot or will not do something, then we won't do it.

> *Excellence*: We are satisfied with nothing less than the very best in everything we do. We will continue to raise the bar for everyone. The great fun here will be for all of us to discover just how good we can really be.

In a 1998 video titled "Vision and Values,"[1] one of the company's top executives says, "It's a tough world out there, a very competitive world. And there probably are times out there where there's a desire to cut corners, but we can't have that...."

"[We are a company] that deals with everyone with absolute integrity," says another corporate executive in the video. "We play by all the rules. We stand by our word. We mean what we say, and we say what we mean. We want people to leave a transaction with [our company] thinking that they have been dealt with in the highest possible way as far as integrity and truthfulness and really doing our business right. ...Like everything else we do, we kind of set the standard."

The message to the outside world couldn't have been clearer: This company's phenomenal success was largely the result of its core values, which had been intentionally integrated into every level of the massive organization.

Fast-forward one year. On December 2, 2001, the company filed for bankruptcy, the largest bankruptcy in history at the time. That company was Enron (in case you haven't already guessed it by now). So much for corporate values aligning with the actions of its leaders and employees, right?

The Values Farce

The story of Enron's fraudulent rise and spectacular fall is well known, particularly the part about the company's emphasis on "vision and values." Those of us who follow business news have long been drawn to this spectacular tale of hubris. What a joke. And then we recall the 25,000 employees, the vast majority of whom were upstanding people of high moral character, people who lived and breathed their company's values but still lost their jobs and their life savings and their retirement money. That part? Not so funny.

Here's the thing—Enron wanted the entire world to know what they supposedly stood for. The "Vision and Values" video made by future felons Ken Lay and Jeffrey Skilling was never intended for the company's employees per se. Instead, its main purpose was to convince the general public of the company's virtue. It was a public-relations stunt, a marketing ploy that had nothing to do with what actually went on *inside* the company; instead, it merely *projected an image to the outside world.*

Although many of the Enrons of the world have been exposed, a large number of companies of all shapes and sizes still do not operate in a manner consistent with the values they espouse. In these organizations, a vast chasm exists between carefully crafted value statements and the reality of how daily business is conducted. Their mission statements, corporate values, and company creeds are merely designed to attract talent and win business.

With few exceptions, a company's founders, board of directors, and C-level executives come up with the company values. They gather behind closed doors to formulate lofty, aspirational phrases and platitudes about who they are and what they believe. Then, after much wrangling, focus grouping, writing, and revising, the doors of the executive suite are thrown open and—like Moses descending from Mount Sinai with the Ten Commandments—the company presents its Core Values. (Cue angelic choir.)

The newly minted values are passed down through the ranks via the company grapevine, newsletter, or town hall meeting to the Israelites—excuse me, the employees—the people who have been performing the actual day-to-day functions of the organization. The grandiose expectation is that these values will magically inspire higher levels of performance, productivity, and loyalty.

You can guess how well such a scenario usually plays out.

Powerful Words Sell, but Employees Aren't Buying

At a time when people yearn for the time-honored values and social mores of the past, words like *integrity, excellence, service, respect,* and *trust* resonate. As consumers, we want to believe that these words mean something, that they're the foundational principles of the company that uses them. We hope the company stands behind them. But the acid test of these claims is in how the company's employees live out those values.

Is the salesman who approaches us on the car lot *friendly* and *honest* or abrasive and slick? Is the plumber *reliable*, or did he arrive 30 minutes late and charge us for a repair that we're not convinced was necessary? And if this restaurant is supposedly dedicated to *cleanliness* and *healthy choices*, why are all the dishes deep fried?

A company's core values mean nothing unless they are embodied and displayed by the people who work at the company. Not just by the well-educated, handsomely paid execs in the corporate office, but by everyone who works for the company. Everyone from the CEO to the mid-level manager to the entry-level staff to the part-time janitor who comes in on weekends.

However, this ethos has become the exception rather than the rule. In 2013, the research firm TINYPulse surveyed 40,000 employees from 300 companies around the world and found that only 42 percent even knew their organization's vision, mission, and values.[2] And if employees don't know their employer's core values, how can those employees behave in accordance with those values?

> A company's core values mean nothing unless they are embodied and displayed by the people who work at the company.

Quite simply, they can't.

In my work with hundreds of organizations, I've come to this conclusion: Truly great workplace cultures are those where the leaders and the employees share the same vision and where their core values and mission are aligned.

Corporate Values in the Wake of High-Profile Meltdowns

The very notion of corporate values is relatively new. What's even newer is (1) the relationship between a company's values and its culture (corporate alignment) and (2) the way a company sees its role and what that role means for those who work at the company (employer and employee alignment).

The Old School view of a company's "role" was pretty straight-forward. In his acclaimed book *Capitalism and Freedom* (1962), Nobel prize-winning economist Milton Friedman summarized the mid-20th-century Old School mindset, noting that "[T]here is one and only one social responsibility of business—to use its resources and engage in activities designed to increase its profits so long as it stays within the rules of the game, which is to say, engages in open and free competition without deception or fraud."[3]

Friedman's matter-of-fact summation of a business' role was the predominant view of an age that seemed to pursue profits at all costs with a near-religious fervor. Back then, owners, executives, and managers felt little inclination to build a company and an associated workplace culture based on a set of corporate ethics or values. The idea probably never occurred to them. Performance and profit were what seemed to matter most. In an attempt to appeal to investors and customers, companies engraved power words on gilt plaques prominently positioned in the lobby of the corporate office. Those same words appeared on the inside cover of the companies' annual reports and on the companies' "about us" pages on their websites.

Then came Enron's fall from grace and the seismic shift that resulted. All of a sudden, values, or a lack thereof, became the talk of the town. In the post-Enron era, smart leaders woke up and took a serious look at who they were and what they actually believed in.

In 2004, in the wake of multiple dramatic corporate collapses, reporters, researchers, bloggers, and others had a lot to say about the need for real corporate values vs. empty words. Around that time, the Aspen Institute and Booz Allen Hamilton released a landmark global study of corporate values that surveyed senior executives at 365 companies in 30 countries in five regions, almost a third of them CEOs or board members. It states:

> If the new attention to values were simply a transi-
> tory reaction to the business scandals of recent years,

or merely a public relations device to direct or deflect media or investor attention, it would be worth little note. But more companies are engaging in these and other values-driven management improvement efforts, including values training, appraising executives and staff on their adherence to values, and retaining organizational experts to help them understand how their values affect performance.[4]

The study then cites some contemporary examples. For instance, during her keynote address at the 2004 Annual Conference of Business for Social Responsibility, Xerox CEO Anne Mulcahy said that "[c]orporate values helped save Xerox during the worst crisis in our history," adding that "living our values" had been a key corporate performance objective.

As another example, in 2002 Dell conducted a massive two-year reexamination of its corporate culture. The result was a new corporate values statement called the "Soul of Dell"—a document that aligned Dell's values with those of their employees by accurately reflecting the views and aspirations of the company's workforce.

These brief examples represent a continuing worldwide trend that reinforces what successful companies increasingly consider to be an imperative link between corporate values—real values vs. Enron-like window dressing—and workplace culture. The New School says that a company's values are much more than an expression of priorities or ethics; they're the markers by which a workforce and executive management go about the business of fulfilling their mission and making a profit. Alignment between employer and employee is key.

Demystifying Corporate Culture

In 2011, global management consulting firm A.T. Kearney released a paper titled "Demystifying Corporate Culture,"[5] in which the authors tackle this idea of values and workforce engagement. As an example of how important leadership is to aligning values with the workforce, they relate a story about Procter & Gamble (P&G) CEO A.G. Lafley, who took the reins of the global business in 2000:

> When A.G. Lafley was appointed CEO in 2000...the company had only a 15 to 20 percent commercial success rate of new brands and products. At the time...[b]rand and product innovation...was considered in-house competency that gave P&G market advantage....
>
> Lafley recognized a need to change. ...To succeed, P&G needed to ensure that innovation reflected deep understanding of customer needs and perceptions, and top executives needed to accelerate the pace of innovation dramatically. This could not be done...unless the entire organization embraced new ways of working. P&G introduced its Connect + Develop strategy, where innovation is developed collaboratively across the organization and with external partners.
>
> The strategy required a culture of trust and open exchange across the organization and with key external players. It required the workforce to make fundamental changes: increased focus on the end customer, greater curiosity and openness to new ideas, and significantly more internal and external collaboration. ...Organization structures, systems, communications and even recruitment reinforced the new culture and the desired behaviors. The result was a closing of the gap between the old thinking and the new innovation-driven strategy and an organization that was aligned for success. Today, P&G's Connect + Develop strategy has resulted in more than 1,000 active agreements with external parties. During Lafley's tenure, sales doubled, profits quadrupled, and the company's market value increased by more than $100 billion.

What value alignment did Lafley need from his team to realize this ambitious plan and completely change the corporate culture? Trust, communication, curiosity, openness, and collaboration. And

> when he infused these values throughout the organization and achieved employee buy-in, he did more than engage his workforce. He helped create a workforce truly committed to trust, communication, curiosity, openness, and collaboration. He helped create a workforce on fire.

Admittedly, the value statements shared by Xerox, Dell, and P&G seem inspirational on the surface. There's nothing inherently wrong with inspirational values so long as they are foundational. However, to have a real impact these foundational values need to be embraced and evidenced by everyone who cashes a company paycheck.

Do Your Values Align with Theirs?

When presenting to leaders and managers, I ask audience members to come up with five adjectives that they would use in a job posting to recruit new employees. To better prepare them for this simple assignment, I tell them that all they need to do is think of the most successful people they have working for them—their "superstars" so to speak—and list the attributes that describe those people.

Regardless of the company or industry, the responses I've heard over the years are strikingly similar. The participants begin shouting out Eagle Scout-worthy character traits like *honest, dedicated, loyal, creative, diligent, responsible, hardworking, team-oriented*, etc.

Next, I ask them to imagine how they think their employees would respond if they were asked to list five adjectives describing the kinds of people who succeed at the company.

I then ask them to compare their list with the one that their employees would compile. "Are the words identical? Somewhat similar? Or are they as different as east is from west?" The more different the two lists, the more divided you are from your people.

True alignment is achieved when your list, your employees' lists, and your company's core values are the same.

Great Companies Align Employees with Core Values

Perfect alignment between leaders and workers is an ambitious goal, but in reality it's unrealistic. However, it's the pursuit of that perfect alignment that keeps great cultures moving forward and constantly improving.

Let's examine how some values-based companies and organizations are aligning their people around their core values.

The Dwyer Group: Using Core Values as the Ultimate Criteria for Every Decision

Headquartered in Waco, Texas, The Dwyer Group is the parent company of eight service-based franchised brands and more than 1,700 franchise partners in nine countries. Former CEO, now Co-Chair, Dina Dwyer-Owens credits her father (the company's founder) with building a company culture centered on company values and employer/employee alignment. "The reason our culture is special is because Don Dwyer had clear expectations in his values," she told me. "No matter who he was talking to—whether it was a franchisee, an employee, or a banker—he always communicated what his expectations were in the relationship and how we were going to do business, and then he would hold us accountable to that." No generic values. No empty mission statements. Just a clear line from the founder down to the employees and franchisees.

"After his death, we wanted to keep this culture special, so we decided to create a code of values so that any one of us knows when we have not lived up to those values," Dina said. "Every employee has the right to hold another employee accountable to the core values. I have asked them to hold me accountable. They can come knock on my door if they feel I have not lived up to a value, and we'll have a talk about it."

The Dwyer Group Code of Values

(Quoted directly from http://www.dwyergroup.com/code-of-values.asp)[6]

Like many companies, The Dwyer Group has an official mission statement and vision; however, unlike most companies, we also have a Code of Values that each employee and franchisee is urged to know and follow by heart and with heart. The Code of Values serves as a set of universal guidelines to which we strive to adhere, from the bottom of the organization all the way to the top. In fact, any meeting of three or more employees of The Dwyer Group begins with a reciting of the Code of Values.

WE LIVE OUR CODE OF VALUES BY...

Respect
> treating others as we would like to be treated.
> listening with the intent to understand what is being said and acknowledging that what is said is important to the speaker.
> responding in a timely fashion.
> speaking calmly and respectfully, without profanity or sarcasm.
> acknowledging everyone as right from their own perspective.

Integrity
> making only agreements we are willing, able and intend to keep.
> communicating any potentially broken agreements at the first appropriate opportunity to all parties concerned.
> looking to the system for correction and proposing all possible solutions if something is not working.
> operating in a responsible manner: "above the line...."
> communicating honestly and with purpose.
> asking clarifying questions if we disagree or do not understand.
> never saying anything about anyone that we would not say to him or her.

Customer Focus
> continuously striving to maximize internal and external customer loyalty.
> making our best effort to understand and appreciate the customers' needs in every situation.

Having Fun in the Process!

Noted Dina, "Our code of values is who we are; it's not just a piece of paper. I've learned that only five percent of companies do anything with their code of values—they're either put up on a wall or tucked away on the shelf. But at The Dwyer Group, we have a system that ensures that our code of values is part of our everyday life."

That's values-based leadership. That's employer/employee alignment. It's not just about accountability; it's about commitment throughout the enterprise. Everyone—from CEO Mike Bidwell and the leadership team to the housekeeper—has a responsibility to uphold the values that govern performance.

Dina also shared with me the organization's policy mandating that whenever three or more associates or franchisees have a meeting of any nature, they must take a few moments beforehand to recite the company values. They can change it up to keep the exercise fresh. Sometimes they recite the values in reverse order or share a favorite value. The key is reinforcing the culture they have created. "Sometimes after reciting the values, the conversation will begin with an associate telling a quick story about how he or she saw Dwyer values come alive in a recent business meeting, phone call, or some act of customer service," she said.

Sound tedious? Redundant? Maybe so. But if you were to recite your wedding vows before you sat down to settle an argument with your spouse, how differently might that conversation go?

That's what Dwyer's Code of Values is all about: Letting values guide decisions. And it doesn't stop there.

The Dwyer Group regularly surveys all employees and Dwyer brand franchisees, asking them to rate their supervisor or franchisor according to the company's four specific values. Their goal is to measure whether the company is living its values from within. In 2013, company supervisors received an average score of 93.8 percent, one point higher than a year earlier. Regarding the increase, Dina remarked, "We still have room for improvement."

Vynamic: Where the Employee Is in Control

In Philadelphia, the City of Brotherly Love, Vynamic headquarters overlooks the famous "LOVE" sculpture set in Love Park across from City Hall.

The location seems appropriate, because Vynamic, an 80-plus-person healthcare consultancy, and its CEO and founder, Dan Calista, seem to never tire of showing the love to their people.

For example, many consultants would openly admit that, while extensive travel often comes with the job, business travel can get old real fast. That's precisely why Vynamic stands out as a firm that goes against that grain. Ranked the number-one most prestigious boutique-consulting firm in the U.S. by IvyExec.com in early 2015 and the number five overall best small firm to work for in the U.S. by *Consulting Magazine*, Vynamic has gone beyond paying competitive salaries—founder and CEO Dan Calista reverse-engineered the organization to take the excessive travel whammy out of the consultants' job description. "We're able to hire the top talent in the industry precisely because we are committed to enabling consultants to be in control of where they work and what they do," Dan said.

That's right. Vynamic not only pays consultants very well but also doesn't force travel upon them. (Such a policy may seem unbelievable to those road warriors who log more time on airplanes than they do in their own homes every year.)

Another of Vynamic's innovations is called zzzMail, an email blackout period. zzzMail has helped to foster a culture of autonomy. In short, Vynamic has a policy that no work emails are to be sent between 10 PM and 6 AM on weekdays. Even more unusual, no work emails are to be sent on weekends. If a critical issue demands a response, employees are encouraged to pick up the phone or send a text. "We really felt that sending emails during late hours or on weekends just led to sleepless nights, which snowballs into more stress at work," Dan said.

Employee control is important to the culture because Dan didn't want to hire people who would come to feel trapped in their jobs with no chance of growing or changing in their roles. That flexibility has shot employee engagement sky high and contributed to a turnover rate of less than 10 percent in the last five years.

Embedded in the Vynamic logo are the words "I am." The "I am Vynamic" message symbolizes Vynamic's values, encourages employees to thrive, and reinforces the freedom they have to apply their unique strengths. The first question Vynamic new hires are asked when they accept a job is this: "What will your Vynamic color be?" As with a fingerprint or a snowflake, each Vynamic employee has a unique Vynamic "I am" color. (The color is managed by Vynamic's creative team to ensure RGB [red, green, blue] uniqueness.) This color is then used in the logo on each employee's business cards and becomes part of each individual's identity. Vynamic even paints each employee's office walls with the employee's distinctive color, which reinforces the employee's unique identity. When you meet someone from Vynamic, ask "What is *your* Vynamic color?" and you'll immediately strike a personal connection.

By ceding control and empowering their employees, Vynamic shows a high level of trust in the team. It's why Dan's able to say, "Everybody wants to hire our people." Indeed, some of the best consultants in the industry line up to work for Vynamic. Having the top consultants in their industry in turn attracts more clients than the company can accommodate. The company is then able to charge top rates for its services, generate ample business without marketing, and have the luxury of turning away those consulting contracts that would force travel upon its consultants. Success has enabled Vynamic to decide which jobs to take based on the needs and concerns of the staff. "What I know is that I want to grow for people, not at the expense of people," Dan said. And in doing so, everybody wins.

Living Up to Their Core Values at BB&T Corp.

Kelly King, Chairman and CEO of financial services firm BB&T Corp., told me about the company's Personal Development Planning Process. Once a year, a "coach" (supervisor) sits down with an associate. In addition to evaluating the associate's performance against clear job-relevant performance objectives, the manager rates the associate based on his or her performance according to the company's values and culture. Not based on sales figures, not based on whether or not they made their financial goals. The question BB&T asks is this: In your job performance, how have you lived up to our core values?

"There has been a shift in our society over the last 20 years or so where there's more of a view toward values," Kelly said. "Many universities are teaching that there is no such thing as absolute honesty—honesty is relative, which is totally contrary to our culture. We do our best to screen new people to see that their values are as aligned with ours as much as possible. We spend a lot of time teaching our beliefs because our culture is very solid, firm, and thick. After some time, you will either find your place or you will leave."

The process is also repeated in reverse. Annually, BB&T conducts a confidential associate survey that accurately measures a range of items that gauge associate engagement. Associates evaluate 55 statements, such as, "I feel valued by BB&T, I have a promising future at BB&T, and I trust our senior leadership." The complete, unedited results of the survey are made available to all associates. In an industry that has faced enormous headwinds, BB&T has remained a top-quartile engaged corporation by sharing with all associates both the strengths and challenges reported through the survey and consistently living up to the company's values.

Kelly stressed that he personally takes ownership in leading BB&T's Strong Associate Value Proposition. "I want to know that our associates truly are proud to work at BB&T," Kelly said. Pride is one of BB&T's core values. "While the vast majority of our associates consistently say in the annual survey that they are proud to work for BB&T, our goal is to reach 100 percent," Kelly enthusiastically told me.

The company also uses "mystery shoppers," a formal program where "shoppers" interact with an associate at a local branch. "It's not to catch someone doing something wrong," Kelly told me. "We want to catch someone doing something right." When that happens, bells go off. It's a celebration—and a vindication that an employee living the corporate values is an engaged employee.

Ben & Jerry's: Values-Led, Not Consumer-Driven

Perhaps more than any other U.S. company, Ben & Jerry's is known for its commitment to social responsibility and civic engagement. CEO Jostein Solheim knows that his company's values aren't shared by everyone. That's why he calls Ben & Jerry's a values-led business. "We're not consumer driven," he said. "We do things that we really passionately believe in and that we believe are the right things to do."

Said Jostein: "I believe it's worth years of work to send a team to a sugar co-op in Latin America to observe their business practices firsthand and make certain they are treating their employees fairly and that they are being good stewards of their resources and the environment. It's important to let the team make the decision as to whether or not Ben & Jerry's is going to buy from this producer rather than simply allowing the co-op to make a presentation in our offices showing PowerPoint slides and a spreadsheet and tell us about what they do in the community." That's values-led leadership. Right down to the basic commodities they put in their ice cream, Ben & Jerry's lives its values every day and in every possible way.

I served as the keynote speaker for several hundred owners and general managers at the 2014 Ben & Jerry's Franchise Convention in Puerto Rico. The convention lasted four days, one of which was spent at a local orphanage where Jostein, the entire leadership team, and every independent franchise owner and general manager spent eight-ten hours painting, trimming trees, and cleaning up and improving the exterior of the grounds. This wasn't a publicity stunt or a teambuilding activity intended to bond independent store owners to their mother ship. It's just who Ben & Jerry's is. Service is an intangible core value deeply woven into their culture.

Jostein told me that when Hurricane Irene hit the U.S. east coast in 2011, 20 percent of the staff at their corporate headquarters in Waterbury, Vermont missed work because they were helping to organize and participate in the relief effort for the flooded town. They didn't just throw money at the problem; they went in with boots on the ground bearing shovels, flashlights, sandbags, and provisions, and they worked from dusk to dawn throughout the recovery efforts. Jostein drove to the eye of the storm, put on his boots and gloves, and joined the effort—he showed up as just another Ben & Jerry's employee there to help the community recover from a devastating storm.

Neither Jostein nor his executive staff had to tell the employees to get involved. They just did. The employees were so aligned with the values of their organization that their actions were exactly what Ben Cohen and Jerry Greenfield would have urged them to do had they been teenaged scoopers at their first store back in 1978.

Lost productivity? Sure. Lost short-term profits? No question. But if value can be placed on the loyalty customers have for a brand and the respect and trust employees have for an employer, then Ben & Jerry's has set the standard.

Five Ways to Ensure ER-EE Core Value Alignment

Leadership coach Ray B. Williams notes, "Values, in a true sense, are basic, fundamental, enduring and meant to be acted upon. In contrast, slogans, platitudes and tag lines are ephemeral, transitory and relative, and often not meant to be taken seriously. For example...who today would believe that part of BP's mission and values are to do no harm to the environment?"[7]

These days, employees and customers alike demand more than lip service. They want to work for and buy from companies that believe in something and live and act according to those beliefs.

Start by creating, revising, or at the very least reviewing your organization's core values. If you're creating or revising them, make certain you involve employees from all departments and at every level in the process.

Next, follow the five-step process described below:

1. **Interview and hire according to your values.** Corporate values have meaning only when they're internalized—believed—by the employees themselves. So start from the beginning. For example, if one of your core values centers on integrity, ask job candidates to describe a situation where their integrity was tested in the workplace and how they responded. Or give them a hypothetical situation and ask them to describe in detail how they would handle it. Refrain from asking yes or no softball questions, like "At ACME, we value integrity. Is that also important to you?" Go the extra mile to make sure they know your company values from the get-go and ask the kinds of questions that reveal whether or not those values align with theirs.

2. **Train around those values.** Sure, your corporate values will be listed in the piles of new hire materials that employees receive, but mention of and reflection upon those values shouldn't stop there. Talk about values throughout your employees' tenures, and give employees constant opportunities to internalize those values.

    Use training opportunities to allow your people to reflect upon hypothetical situations and real-world examples. A company that puts a heavy emphasis on reliability should reinforce that value in each and every phase of its operation. A package delivery service, for example, might promote the following value: "When it snows, our building maintenance staff is called in two hours early to clear the lots so that there are no weather-related delays in getting our drivers out of our docks and on the road." Repetition throughout the training process ensures that your organization's core values are engrained throughout all phases of your operation.

3. **Discipline employees who don't honor the values, and reward those who do.** One of the best ways to show that your values really mean something is to recognize and praise employees who honor those values and reprimand and discipline those who disregard them. Acknowledge and reward employee behaviors that embody your corporate values; make certain that those employees—and their coworkers—understand they are being praised because they have demonstrated core value alignment. "Because you demonstrated XYZ's commitment to above-and-beyond service in your recent interaction with ACME Corp., we have arranged to

have your car receive a complete auto service and detailing."

When your people honor the company's values, call it out. And when they don't, be sure to let them know that too. Always, always, always link values to performance.

4. **Evaluate performance in accordance with core values.** Every employee review should include—if not narrowly focus on—how the individual is performing according to the company's core values. Doing so ties aspirational words and phrases on the walls of the corporate headquarters to the specific actions and behaviors of the people who are expected to live up to those values.

5. **Model behaviors.** No matter what those wall plaques say, your employees will do as you and your managers do. Take your company's values seriously every single day, and your employees will follow. Ignore those values or treat them as mere suggestions to be disregarded at whim, and employees will do the same. Make business decisions based on your beliefs, then make sure you communicate to staff how those decisions reflect the corporate values you all live by. Make sure they see that you walk the talk.

Repetition throughout the training process ensures that your organization's core values are engrained throughout all phases of your operation.

If your values reflect the person you are and the company you've built, then your employees will respond. They'll respect those values and want to live them, or they will find employment elsewhere. As BB&T's Kelly King noted, "After some time, you will either conform or you will leave." In time, your company will fit your employees to a tee, and vice versa. And that's a very good thing.

When Values Collide with Profits, Great Companies Stand by Their Values

Chick-fil-A restaurants engage in a costly practice that none of their main competitors are willing to match: They close on Sundays. Although they could substantially increase profits by being open seven days a week, Chick-fil-A believes their employees should have one day away from work where they can rest, spend time with family and friends, and worship if they choose to do so.

On October 1, 2014, **CVS** retail drug stores gained nationwide attention when they stopped selling cigarettes in their 7,700 retail outlets, consciously choosing health over profits. Industry analysts say that decision will cost them $2 billion in lost sales each year. "We've got 26,000 pharmacists and nurse practitioners who are helping millions of patients each and every day," said Larry Merlo, CEO of CVS Caremark. "They manage conditions like high blood pressure, high cholesterol, and diabetes—all conditions that are worsened by smoking. We've come to the decision that cigarettes have no place in an environment where healthcare is being delivered."[8]

In April 2014, **Amazon.com** launched a Pay to Quit program to entice unhappy or disengaged employees to jump ship. Once each year, Amazon offers its fulfillment center employees a cash incentive to leave the company. The offer is $2,000 for the first year, and the amount increases $1,000 each year after that up to a maximum of $5,000. Amazon isn't forcing employees to leave, it's just giving an incentive to those who feel less than elated to be working for the organization. The program thins the herd, leaving behind only truly satisfied, dedicated workers who are eager to serve their customers.

Many outdoor clothing manufacturers promote environmentalism, but few can match the dedication of **Patagonia**. In 1985, Patagonia launched "1% for the Planet," donating one percent of their annual profits to environmental causes, and they publically encourage other companies to join them in this mission. And it doesn't stop there. Recognizing the impact that the manufacturing of outerwear products has on the planet, Patagonia actually asks consumers to refrain from purchasing their line of products unless they truly need them.

Omni Hotels made a costly decision in 1999. Several prominent media-based tech companies had begun offering large hotel chains a deal that most couldn't refuse. In exchange for allowing them to promote a lineup of pay-per-view movies to hotel guests, the tech companies would pay for and install a new, state-of-the-art television in each guest room. With these TVs and cabling packages costing an average of $400 each, hotels that took advantage of the offer could save tens or even hundreds of thousands of dollars. However, when Omni's owners learned that pornographic movies would be included in the movie offerings to their guests, they turned down the lucrative deal.

Your Values Are Always on Display for Your Employees...and Your Customers

Organizational values matter now more than ever. Consumers have an incredible number of choices in the marketplace, and while price is always a factor, many customers want to do business with companies that share their values. Likewise, today's best and brightest employees are in demand, and they want to work for companies and organizations that align with their values.

It doesn't matter how impressive your company values appear when displayed in the lobby of your headquarters. The only thing that matters is how your organization actually functions, how it goes about its daily business, and, most importantly, what guiding principles serve as the foundation for the important decisions made throughout your company each and every day.

Your company is on display. It's no secret how your company treats employees, customers, vendors, suppliers, and others. With the Internet, social media, 24/7 news channels, and the plethora of smart phones with built-in hi-def video cameras, the world has a ringside seat.

With your core values always on display, it's to your advantage to strive for perfect alignment between the words on the engraved plaque in your boardroom and the attitudes, beliefs, and behaviors of the people on the front lines of your business.

Igniters, Flamethrowers, and Burnout Extinguishers

The suggestions and questions below are for leaders looking to create or change the values that help define who they are and why they do what they do. How do you want to run your business? This is a critical question.

Your company is on display. It's no secret how your company treats employees, customers, vendors, suppliers, and others—the world has a ringside seat.

When you start thinking about the questions below in an honest, no-nonsense way, you'll pinpoint a set of values that helps you commit yourself more fully to the company you've helped develop. Remember: If you don't believe in the ambitions and dreams that went into building your organization, you stand little chance of getting others to believe in them (and even less of a chance of building a workforce that's on fire).

1. **Reflect on the values of your organization.** Ask yourself these questions:

    ⚲ Does your organization live by a set of values that helps you, your managers, and your employees get things done?

    ⚲ Are your values more than a plaque on the boardroom wall? Are they a living set of principles that guide the actions and behaviors of everyone throughout the organization?

    ⚲ Do your employees know your corporate values by heart? Even the hourly part-time people in the non-sexy or low-skill positions?

◊ What event or events (large or small) happened today at the office that epitomized your company's values or, conversely, threw them out the window? (If your answer is "I can't think of a thing that epitomized my company's values," then ask yourself why that is.)

2. **Make sure your values and your corporate values align**. If you're a leader or a manager at an established company whose corporate values are etched in stone, then you might feel powerless to revamp those values. If that's the case, then it's important—critical even—that you are in full alignment with your company's values. That doesn't mean you should turn a blind eye to values with which you disagree. Far from it. However, it does mean that those values will feel hollow if you don't really believe them. Hollow values are problem values, the kinds that can lead to big challenges down the road.

3. **Walk the front lines**. Ask the VP, the CFO, the team lead, managers at every level, employees in every department and division, the receptionist, the janitor, the security guard in the lobby, and the mailroom clerk to recite your company's core values. If any of them give you a blank stare, your organization is out of alignment. Make fixing it a priority.

4. **Write your own company obituary**. Imagine your company is going out of business after a long and successful tenure. What would you want the article to say about your company? What would you want long-time customers to say? Your employees?

5. **Craft values you believe in—values you and your team can live by**. Create values that don't currently

exist or overhaul existing values if those values are flexible or in flux. And then share those values with your employees. Ask for their input. Take their responses seriously.

6. **Model the right behaviors.** If someone watched you at work for a week or two and then listed what they thought the company values were based upon your actions, how accurate would their assessment be? Before you make an important decision, review your company's values. Remember, *employees will abide by their employer's values about as seriously as the employer abides by them him or herself.*

7. **Inspire your team.** If you know your company isn't doing enough to live its values, start with yourself and your team. Ask yourself: What can I do today that lives up to my company's values, and how can I inspire my team to emulate my actions?

8. **Differentiate yourself from the competition.** What can you say about your company culture and your people that your competitors can't say about theirs? Every company says that they have great people, that they focus on quality, that safety matters, that they put people first, etc. So get specific. What truly distinguishes your company from others in your industry?

9. **Get creative.** When three or more Dwyer Group associates or franchisees meet, they take a few moments beforehand to recite the company values. What creative ideas do you have for reinforcing your company's values throughout the ranks?

10. **Take the test.** If your employees rated their supervisors according to whether or not they live the company's values from within, what average score do you

think those supervisors would receive? What score would you find satisfactory, and what exactly are you willing to do to help your supervisors (and the company as a whole) achieve that score?

Notes

1. Enron, "Vision and Values," accessed February 23, 2015, http://www .youtube.com/watch?v=tc-l9J6WiMY.

2. TINYpulse, "7 Vital Trends Disrupting Today's Workplace," TINYpulse.com Engagement Survey, accessed February 23, 2015, https://www.tinypulse.com/employee-engagement-survey-2013.

3. Milton Friedman, *Capitalism and Freedom* (Chicago, IL: University of Chicago Press, 1962), 133.

4. Chris Kelly, Paul Kocourek, Nancy McGaw, and Judith Samuelson, "Deriving Value from Corporate Values," The Aspen Institute and Booz |Allen | Hamilton, 2005, accessed February 23, 2015, https:// www.aspeninstitute.org/sites/default/files/content/docs/bsp/ VALUE%2520SURVEY%2520FINAL.PDF.

5. Ira Gaberman, Ingrid Devoi, Kevin Crump, and Marieke Witjes, "Demystifying Corporate Culture: Why People Do What They Do," A.T. Kearney, Inc., 2011, accessed February 23, 2015, http://www .atkearney.com/documents/10192/379971/Demystifying_Corporate _Culture1.pdf/5d0f4c04-8fbe-4f7b-8fda-7e0a74c49f0e.

6. The Dwyer Group, "Code of Values," accessed February 23, 2015, http://www.dwyergroup.com/code-of-values.asp.

7. Ray B. Williams, "Why Most Corporate Value Statements Are Meaningless," in Wired for Success, *Psychology Today*, June 25, 2013.

8. Matthew Harper, "Kicking the Habit: CVS to Stop Selling Tobacco, Sacrificing $2 Billion in Sales for Public Health and Future Growth," Forbes, February 5, 2014, http://www.forbes.com/sites/ matthewherper/2014/02/05/cvs-to-stop-selling-tobacco-sacrificing-2 -billion-in-sales-for-public-health-and-future-growth/.

Chapter Four

ATMOSPHERE: Ensuring Your Employees Are Safe, Well-Equipped, *and Goofing Off!*

Shaped like the blade of an axe, standing 726 feet high, and weighing more than 18 Empire State buildings combined, the Hoover Dam is a jaw-dropping wonder of the industrial world. Composed of enough concrete to pave a 16-foot highway from San Francisco to New York City, this behemoth construction provides flood control, irrigation, drinking water, and electricity to more than 20 million people in Nevada, Arizona, and California.

The Hoover Dam was built between 1931 and 1935 by a consortium of six major tunnel, railroad, and highway contractors that went by the name Six Companies. This conglomeration had submitted the winning bid of $49 million dollars, equal to nearly $1 billion in today's economy. The promise of above-average wages (between 50 cents to $1.25 an hour) drew more than 42,000 men to the Nevada desert in search of work. However, it took a total workforce of only 21,000 to complete the massive project in less than five years, and it came in under budget.

At any given time throughout its construction, approximately 3,500 workers were onsite, most working eight-hour days and seven-day weeks in temperatures ranging from freezing cold to 119-degree blazing heat.

Now, Six Companies was under stiff pressure to meet the government's deadlines or face exorbitant fines. These expectations caused management to disregard many commonsense safety precautions in favor of speed, forcing beleaguered workers to move at a furious pace even when their health and safety were at extreme risk. Not only did workers have to endure extreme variances in temperatures, but they also had to contend with the ever-present dangers of carbon monoxide poisoning, dehydration, and electrocution, just to name a few. Aside from the hundreds of serious injuries that occurred while building the dam, 96 workers lost their lives in accidents ranging from dynamite blasting to drowning to falling off ledges and platforms to being trampled by the heavy construction equipment.

When the working conditions became unbearable, Six Companies' workforce went on strike. However, in the midst of the Great Depression workers knew they'd better not stay out of work too long or they'd be replaced by a steady stream of other men who would gladly take their jobs. Shortly after the strike began, the worker's demands were rejected by both the dam supervisor and the U.S. Secretary of Labor. Not surprisingly, the workers returned to the jobsite without a new agreement.

An enjoyable workplace atmosphere was not a top-of-mind concern for the Hoover Dam workers, who were focused on getting a paycheck. The only people who thought less about workplace atmosphere and job conditions were the leaders and managers of Six Companies. If you were lucky enough to land one of those Dam jobs (pardon the pun), you'd better keep your head down, shut your mouth, and do that job perfectly. And if you became ill or, worse, got injured on the job, you had better not let anyone find out, as your job would be filled by someone else in a flash.

Of course, that was then and this is now. These days, the pendulum has swung so far in the other direction that it's now the employers who are doing the groveling. Skilled, experienced workers are in short supply and high demand, and the available talent pool seems to grow more shallow with each passing day.

The result? Key employees in your business are perpetually pursued by headhunters, recruiters, and competing employers. The bait most commonly used to lure them away is a sizable bump in pay. And if money alone won't get them to jump, an offer involving a better workplace atmosphere might just do the trick.

Think of Atmosphere as the Rings of Saturn

The entire concept of workplace atmosphere can seem somewhat nebulous. What one might consider a great atmosphere could seem dreadful or repulsive to someone else. Perhaps it's all just a matter of personal taste. And while some cultures are playful and almost circus-like and others are stark and sterile, all work and no play, two key questions remain: Which cultures are the most productive and profitable, and what exactly constitutes an effective workplace atmosphere?

One thing is certain: The atmosphere at your workplace is far too important to be left up to chance or happenstance. Atmosphere is a choice. It must be deliberate.

To better understand atmosphere as a cultural pillar, allow me to use an analogy.

Imagine your company as if it's the planet Saturn. As the Supreme Ruler of Saturn (c'mon, run with me on this…), your goal is to attract the best talent in the universe and to have that talent end up liking the place so much that they'll stay as long as you want them to stay. And while they're there, you're going to want those people to be *on fire* for Saturn, investing themselves as fully as if they themselves were the planet's Supreme Rulers.

The best talent (and, to an extent, even those who may not be highly skilled but can still play an important role in your planet's survival) won't just land on your planet or stay for any period of time just because you want them or need them. In this universe, good people are in demand and can take the opportunity to land on any of the many other stars and planets out there. The people you want most have many other options and are going to weigh the pros and cons of each of the seven rings surrounding your particular planet, ultimately asking one simple question associated with each ring. If the answer to that question is a resounding "yes!" they'll proceed to the next ring. But if the answer is anything but affirmative, the chances are that they'll leave your atmosphere in search of another.

Here are seven rings, in order, followed by the underlying question employees ponder:

1.   **The Safety Ring**: No matter how attractive your planet may appear from afar, employees are not going to want to land there—or stay there—if they feel that their health and safety are not a top priority. They aren't

going to risk life and limb just to build a big dam so that their employer can meet a deadline. While they may accept work that carries certain health risks, they won't give *on-fire* performance, much less engage with any employer they feel hasn't taken every possible precaution to eliminate or greatly minimize the risks associated with the job.

> **EMPLOYEES WONDER:** *Is my employer doing everything possible to keep me safe?*

2.   **The Acceptance Ring**: Today's most successful business leaders understand the importance of employing a diverse workforce. Companies that use a one-size-fits-all approach to hiring and managing people appeal only to the clones and the droids in the mainstream, and they're getting crushed by companies that aren't stuck following dated follow-the-leader practices. Diversity guards against groupthink and promotes innovation and collaboration. Leading organizations actually seek out the outliers and the non-conformists, who, in turn, need assurance from their employer that they can be themselves without fear of being harassed, taunted, teased, and bullied in the workplace. A winning workplace culture in today's rapidly changing world is one where an atmosphere of diversity is embraced, promoted, and protected.

> *Companies that use a one-size-fits-all approach to hiring and managing people appeal only to the clones and the droids in the mainstream, and they're getting crushed by companies that aren't stuck following dated follow-the-leader practices.*

EMPLOYEES WONDER: *Can I be my authentic self while I'm at work?*

3. **The Tool Ring:** The tool ring refers to anything and everything employees need to perform their jobs in the most productive, efficient way possible. In today's fast-paced, high-tech world, last year's best laptops are next year's museum relics. Employees need the right tools, training, and technology at their disposal in order to do their jobs effectively. Whether the tool needed is a special wrench, an all-wheel-drive vehicle with studded snow tires, a lightning-fast Internet connection, protective eyewear and a helmet, an office chair with lumbar support, a digital thermometer, or a tablet running the latest and greatest software, people want to work for a company that consistently provides them with everything they need—or could possibly use—to do their jobs to the best of their abilities.

   EMPLOYEES WONDER: *Do I have everything I need to excel in this job?*

4. **The Boss Ring:** It's often said that employees don't quit their jobs, they quit their boss. A sales rep who's in a slump needs encouragement and coaching to turn things around. Employees with a sick child want a boss who insists they go home and care for their kid. It's impossible to overstate the importance a boss plays in the way employees view their workplace atmosphere. No matter how great the company, the paycheck, the health plan, or the job title, if the boss is a jerk, a quirk, or just plain nonexistent, an employee isn't going to stick around for very long. That's not to say that a manager or supervisor has to be buddy-buddy with employees. It does mandate,

however, that the boss is compassionate, knowledge-able, accessible, fair, and supportive. That's a tall order for anyone. Then again, no one said being a manager was a walk in the park.

EMPLOYEES WONDER: *Do I like, respect, and trust my boss?*

5. **The Coworker Ring**: With few exceptions, employees have little input on company personnel decisions. Employees have to work alongside their coworkers, some of whom they like and some they don't. When people have an extreme personality conflict with a co-worker, they cower and retreat, confront the coworker and create chaos, or start looking for an escape hatch. Similarly, when they find themselves in an environment where they truly like the people they work with and form solid friendships with the people on their team, they tend to remain in their jobs even when better jobs come calling. *On-fire* cultures foster camaraderie and teambuilding so coworkers develop strong bonds and work toward common goals.

    EMPLOYEES WONDER: *Do I genuinely like the people I work with day in and day out?*

6. **The Sensory Ring**: Sight, sound, smell, taste, and touch. The information we gather through our five senses can attract us to our surroundings or repel us. An engaging workplace atmosphere is one where sensory stimuli aren't left up to chance but are instead carefully choreographed and orchestrated. Reflect back on the best-ever and worst-ever jobs you've had, and consider how the sensory environments of each affected your performance. Did you love or hate the music that was piped in? What color were the walls?

Were you always wishing you could open a window, or did you need to put on extra layers just to stay warm? Did the scent of fresh-brewed coffee bring a smile to your face, or were you repulsed by the smell of the chemical cleaners the janitorial services used on the floors each night? The best workplace atmospheres appeal to employees' senses and incorporate a physical layout that encourages interaction.

> **EMPLOYEES WONDER:** *Does this environment energize me or make me want to find an escape hatch?*

7. **The Fun Ring**: Search the job postings on Monster.com, LinkedIn, SimplyHired.com, or other major employment sites, and you'll find that most pepper their job postings with workplace descriptions like *"a fun place to work"* and *"a relaxed, enjoyable atmosphere."* Unlike those 42,000 men who headed to southern Nevada looking for work in 1931, today's job seekers expect to have some fun *while* they're at work, not just at the local watering hole *after* work. But as we'll discuss throughout this chapter, fun doesn't just happen. In fact, making a workplace fun takes a whole lot of work.

> **EMPLOYEES WONDER:** *Are we having any fun around here?*

Does the End Justify the Means?

Because people are different, they'll pass through the rings surrounding your atmosphere at various speeds, intervals, and sequences based on what they value most. However, it's doubtful that anyone who has options (and those are the only people you want in your organization) will ever be attracted to your company—or remain at your company—if one or more of those rings are seriously damaged. And even if they would remain, they wouldn't be engaged employees, much less *on fire* for you. Atmosphere is that important.

At this point, you might be thinking, *"Okay, let me get this straight. I have to provide a compelling atmosphere for my people by making absolutely certain that their safety is a number-one priority and that they will be accepted and embraced as individuals without being subjected to bullying or harassment. I have to make sure that they have the best up-to-date, state-of-the-art tools and equipment available to do their jobs. Oh, and I need to ensure that each employee reports to someone who is compassionate, knowledgeable, accessible, fair, and supportive—and that they work on a team with people they genuinely like and appreciate. I also need to make sure that they're as comfortable as possible. Finally, I must go out of my way to provide opportunities for relaxation, amusement, enjoyment, and a whole lot of fun as they make their way through the workday. You're saying I have to do all that, right, Chester?"*

Yep. That's precisely what I'm saying.

It may sound difficult, and to be honest, it is. But the payoff is huge.

Diversity in the workplace is more pronounced than ever before, and different people like different kinds of workplace atmospheres. And even if you're able to create the perfect atmosphere for all your people today, tomorrow new people will arrive, and who knows what they're going to want. Because the people you have today will have different tastes, opinions, whims, and desires tomorrow, your atmosphere needs to be fluid, not rigid. The trick is to never stop trying to create the best possible cultural atmosphere. It's not about perfection but rather *the pursuit of perfection* that lets people know how much their happiness matters to you.

The Firehouse Subs Family Reunion

Firehouse Subs gets it when it comes to company-wide events. For instance, Firehouse Subs doesn't hold a yearly company picnic or convention; instead, they host a "family reunion," and all attendees are encouraged to bring their spouses and children. The reunion's opening night begins with a spectacular carnival featuring arcade games, jumping castles, live music, strolling entertainers, and dancing, along with more food, drink, and prizes than you'll find at a county fair. There's even a dunk tank where employees can plunge their managers into the water for a few laughs.

For Don Fox, CEO of Firehouse of America LLC, striding over to the dunking booth in his swim trunks is just another day with family.

"I will say," Don said with a laugh, "that I really watched my diet for about a month before I did it."

The following days of the reunion include general sessions and interactive breakout sessions for franchisees. However, there's also a full array of activities running concurrently for toddlers, kids, teens, and spouses, making everyone who attends feel as if they have a place within the Firehouse Subs family.

Boredom: The Archenemy of an On-Fire Atmosphere

A 2013 poll of 500 workers found that more than three out of four employees (77 percent) regret the career choice they made. Of those, more than a third (35 percent) admit to being just plain bored at work.[1] These numbers suggest two important things. First up is the obvious: Many employees are not just disengaged but actually dislike how they spend the better part of their workday.

The second point isn't so obvious. As it turns out, regret can be a *huge* motivator for change. According to cognitive behavioral therapist Dr. Isabelle Bauer, regret can "push people to rectify their mistakes, amend bad behaviors, and spring into action when they are falling short of important goals. ...Put simply, feeling bad, or regretful, may serve as an important impetus for adaptive actions that might not occur otherwise."[2] Said another way, regretful, bored employees may soon become former employees.

Of course, managers can't do much about employee regret. They aren't life coaches or psychiatrists after all. If an employee is truly unhappy in his or her present job, then your office could be Willy Wonka's Chocolate Factory and it won't make much difference in the end. But there is something that employers and managers can do about regret's less intractable cousin, boredom.

The most insidious of employee maladies, boredom can be toxic to an office culture because it can manifest itself in any number of destructive ways. In 2012, researchers at Montclair State University and the University of South Florida completed a study on the link between counterproductive work behavior and boredom. They found six key ways bored employees might harm their organizations—abuse of others, "production deviance" (purposely failing at tasks), sabotage, withdrawal, theft, and horseplay. One of the study's authors told CNN that of these, withdrawal is the most common and shows itself through several familiar "disengaged" habits like calling in sick, showing up late, and taking numerous long breaks.[3]

*The trick is to never stop trying to create the best possible cultural atmosphere. It's not about perfection but rather **the pursuit of perfection** that lets people know how much their happiness matters to you.*

The Old School mentality of workplace atmosphere was borderline inhumane. Think of the workers employed by Six Companies or the old textile factories in the south with row after row of beleaguered workers performing the same task all day, every day. Slacking off on the job was a fireable offense, as was taking more than your allotted 30 minutes for lunch. Employees were expected to work from the moment they arrived to the moment they left, and the mere thought of a company-sponsored holiday party or an employee barbeque in the summer was as inconceivable to them as a 3D printer.

We know better now (at least for the most part). Still, filling the office with a sense of energy or excitement or even joy is a bridge that spans a little too far for some employers. The fact is that creating a fun workplace atmosphere—a place where people actually want to be—is serious business. It takes work to put the fun in work.

But just because it's hard doesn't mean it has to be complicated.

I Got Zapped at Zappos

I recently had the privilege of taking a tour of Zappos and speaking with several of the company's top leaders. Mine was not the popular tour open to the public but rather a behind-the-scenes peek at the wizardry of this renowned workplace culture. (The company's iconic brand is so revolutionary that it was featured on an ABC News 20/20 Report that brought in Barbara Walters to investigate.)

I've read the best-selling business book *Delivering Happiness* written by Zappos' CEO Tony Hsieh, and I've seen some of the clever Zappos employee videos on YouTube, so I wasn't shell-shocked at the sight of the company's nontraditional workplace environment. The converted city hall building in downtown Las Vegas that serves as HQ radiates individuality and personality with a spattering of controlled chaos thrown in for good measure.

The moment you pass through the courtyard and enter the campus, you hear upbeat music pumping through the speakers and see employees engaged in recreational activities. When you step inside the 10-story building, you're immersed in a setting that looks as if a college fraternity has just raided Pee-Wee's Playhouse. There are free snacks and refreshment stations on every floor, and the cafeteria features low-cost (and even some no-cost) food options. And as far as the employee dress code...well, beyond wearing an ID badge, one doesn't seem to exist.

In a word, it's weird...and it doesn't take a gumshoe to see why employees, especially their Millennial employees, truly *love* working at Zappos. There are, however, some less-publicized facets of the Zappos culture that set them apart from traditional employers.

For example, Tony Hsieh's desk is the exact same size and model as those used by all the rest of the employees. And the door to his office is always open because there literally is no door. In fact, none of the top execs are walled off from other employees, and their admins (or "time ninjas") sit within a few feet of them. The management style is a holacracy by design, and the atmosphere sends a clear message that we're all here for the same reason—and that no one in this operation is more important than anyone else.

In addition, I saw several hammocks near one of the call center areas. That's because Zappos managers expect all their call center reps to be alert and enthusiastic while at their desks. If they're not, the managers encourage them to take a break and recharge their batteries in one of the comfy hammocks provided nearby.

These are just a few of the many unusual rings of Zappos that help connect employees to their growing company, to their jobs, and to their millions of happy customers.

Using Diversion to Fight Boredom and Reengage the Disengaged

In the popular television show *The Office,* Jim Halpert is a sales representative at the Scranton, Pennsylvania branch of paper distribution company Dunder Mifflin. Although a decent enough employee (he actually receives numerous promotions throughout the series), Jim struggles in a small-office environment where his colleagues are either disengaged or dull (in some cases both) and where his boss, Michael Scott, lacks any discernible management skills. It's all Jim can do to not go crazy. To break the day-to-day monotony, Jim turns to humor. He regularly pranks his pseudo-nemesis, the über-serious Dwight Schrute, and takes great joy in teasing the earnest and often misguided Michael, whose management style leaves something to be desired.

To say that Jim is a positive force in the office is perhaps going a bit too far. Rather, we might say that Jim relies on his innate sense of humor to liven up the dreariness of the Scranton office and make the workday bearable.

Meanwhile, Michael tries to imbue the office with a certain playfulness and joviality. His number-one goal is to have fun. However, it's exactly because Michael's motives are so transparent and his attempts so bumbling that he loses the one thing a manager should never lose—authority.

Were this a real office, it's doubtful anyone would be around by the second season, much less the ninth and final season. Nevertheless, *The Office* was a successful series in large part because viewers sympathized with the characters and their workplace situations. In a similar manner, audiences have connected with the comic strip *Dilbert* and the movie *Office Space* because they expose the absurdity of many office environments. All of which is kind of sad because it suggests that many offices aren't too far off from companies like Dunder Mifflin or Initech (from *Office Space*).

As it is, shows like *The Office* offer a slightly distorted mirror of the places we work (or have worked in the past). We love *The Office* and *Dilbert* and *Office Space* (and quote liberally from them) because we can laugh at situations similar to the ones we ourselves have experienced.

Employers need to continually ask if they have planned enough positive diversions throughout the year, the month, the week, and even the day to make work something employees truly enjoy.

Diversions in the workplace help to break the monotony of the workday. With few exceptions, most people at work are like Jim Halpert, in spirit if not in action. As we'll soon see, the trick is to channel your employees' innate desire for diversion toward a productive end. Your employees are going to create diversions anyway, so think of it as your job to make sure those diversions ultimately increase rather than decrease productivity.

Let Jim Be Jim

In *The Office,* Jim Halpert breaks the monotony of his day by amusing himself and his coworkers. We all do this (even if we all don't move a colleague's workstation into the bathroom as Jim once did to poor Dwight).

Your employees are going to create diversions anyway, so think of it as your job to make sure those diversions ultimately increase rather than decrease productivity.

With few exceptions, most workers find themselves combating boredom in the routine elements of their jobs. From solitaire to Facebook, from crosswords to online shopping, from pranking officemates to daydreaming, we humans have an innate capacity to purposely divert our attention in order to relieve stress or to put off doing those things we don't want to do.

The fact is that your employees will find ways to entertain themselves from work, and the best diversion is having a little fun. And nothing you do will change that. Take away access to their favorite Internet sites, and they'll turn to their smartphones. Restrict the use of smartphones, and they'll play hockey in the hallways with brooms and rolls of masking tape. And if all else fails, they'll simply daydream through their shift, in which case they're not only being unproductive but also associating work with mind-numbing boredom and fatigue. That's why you shouldn't get rid of your office Jims.

As a leader, you're faced with a simple choice: Ignore the diversions; try to stamp them out, Old School style (and let your employees' predilection for amusement work itself out in potentially damaging ways); *or let Jim be Jim.*

Letting Jim be Jim doesn't mean you need to turn a blind eye to people who waste time. It doesn't mean you look away as your employees spend their days racking up top scores on Words with Friends or online Texas hold 'em.

Rather, letting Jim be Jim empowers Jim's need for diversion, redirecting it toward productive ends—in this case, the company's need for happier employees who look forward to coming to work because it's anything but boring. Great companies go out of their way to provide diversions for employees. In fact, they want the Jims of the world to have a heavy hand in the actual design of the workspace.

The Googles of the world provide loads of ridiculous office perks—gourmet food, onsite state-of-the-art fitness facilities, video games, and ping pong tables, etc.—because they demand a lot from their people and know that diversions are necessities rather than luxuries in today's workplace. But by no means are Google perks the only perks that work. (And some would argue that too many toys instills a sense of obligation in employees, who feel indebted to the company that gives them so much, causing them to work too many long hours and burn out more quickly.)

But few organizations have the resources of a Google. Few organizations can afford elaborate perks and crazy cool diversions. What then?

This is where your Jims can help you substitute creativity for capital.

Accounting 101

Some years ago, I toured an accounting firm in Denver, where I was greeted by Judy, the office receptionist. As it turns out, Judy is also the ultimate ambassador for the company.

On the wall behind her were three *Denver Business Journal* "Best Place to Work in Denver" plaques. Pointing to the plaques, I asked Judy, "What makes this the best place to work in all of Denver?"

"It's the most fun job in the world," she beamed. "We're always pulling pranks on each other, so you never know what's going to happen. Not too long ago they put a new cappuccino machine in the break room. Someone taped a sign on it that said 'Voice Activated.' Then we tried desperately not to bust a gut as unsuspecting employees actually spoke to the machine. When nothing happened, some thought it was malfunctioning and started yelling at it. They didn't even stop to notice there wasn't any kind of a microphone. It's amazing what you can get people to do with a Post-It note and a Sharpie."

At this point, I started to laugh. "Tell me more."

Judy couldn't wait: "From the top down, most of us believe that April Fool's Day should be a national holiday. Everyone is a perpetrator, and everyone is a victim. A couple of years ago we completely filled our boss's car with those Styrofoam packing peanuts. That was payback for a crank call he made and a bogus memo he sent to all employees. And this doesn't even scratch the surface!"

She went on to give a half dozen other reasons why the firm was the best place to work in Denver, each reason backed by enthusiastic examples. When I asked how long she had worked there, she told me, "Fifteen years and counting. I love it!"

The company in question is EKS&H, 500 people strong and rapidly growing. Intrigued by what I heard, I decided to dig deeper. I spoke to an EKS&H employee who said that he joined the firm in December 2004, coming from one of the Big Four accounting firms. At the time, he had no intention of staying very long. "If you told me I'd still be here after all this time, I'd say you're crazy." Today, ten years after he started, he still has no intention of ever leaving—though it's not like he hasn't had the opportunity. Despite offers for more money, he says simply: "For the life of me, I can't think of anywhere else I'd rather work."

Now, we're talking about an accounting firm here. With all due respect, who in their right mind grows up wanting to be an accountant? It seems like the kind of job that one falls into because of a natural talent for number crunching—only after one's dreams of playing point guard in the NBA have been dashed, of course.

Atmosphere is something you expect at Disney, at an amusement park or an entertainment venue. But there's nothing fun about accounting, right?

That's what makes EKS&H a complete and total departure from the norm. The company has hit *The Denver Business Journal's* Best Place to Work list so many times that they took them out of contention and grandfathered them into their hall of fame.

So, yes, there really is a fun accounting firm. At EKS&H, a fun atmosphere isn't just a way to break the monotony of dreary accounting work. It's a must-have. It allows the company to draw some of the most talented financial minds in the industry and compete head to head with the Big Four. Ask around Denver, and you'll find that EKS&H has built a reputation for being *the kind of place where people want to work.*

Let's shift gears for a second. Pick any job in the world, and there are people doing it who wish they weren't. And yet there they are, working day in and day out because, like most of us, they have bills to pay. Even those fortunate folks who are doing exactly what they want to be doing still need a break from work every now and then.

The middle-of-the-road folks—the Steak Knives—might be content at their jobs, but they're still working for the weekend. Come 5:00 PM Friday, they bolt out the door like a herd of elephants. Then for two blissful days they do the things *they want to be doing* before trudging back to work on Monday. The underlying truth of this scenario leaves the employer in a bind. Is work/life balance the solution, the tried and true formula for making the unpleasant, pleasant?

According to Bob Hottman, founding partner and CEO at EKS&H, the answer to that question is "no."

"We don't talk about work/life balance," Bob told me. "At EKS&H, we talk about work/life success."

The reason is actually pretty simple. See, the word *balance* often represents something neutral or passive. You can have work/life balance even when work and life both stink. Hating your job and hating your life outside your job are arguably quite balanced, all the more so if the time you spend doing both is fairly evenly distributed.

Now success—well, that's a different story. There's nothing passive about that. It's a theme that goes to the heart of EKS&H's approach toward its employees. Bob and his colleagues set out to create a firm "where people want to work." Seems simple, except, again, we're talking about an accounting firm here. But Bob and the other partners knew that if they could *get the atmosphere right, then the right employees would want to work there.*

Atmosphere as an Art Form

So how does an accounting firm become a fun place to work? How did they get the atmosphere so right?

For starters, the seven floors at EKS&H are each subdivided into neighborhoods, and each neighborhood has a nickname given to it by the 20–30 associates who "live" in it. There's the Barrio, the Cellar Dwellers, Margaritaville, etc. The neighborhoods are just one way to turn an office into a community. As Bob said, "We try to think small, even though we are reasonably big."

> "We don't talk about work/ life balance. At EKS&H, we talk about work/life success."
> —BOB HOTTMAN,
> Managing Partner, EKS&H

For instance, EKS&H's neighborhoods actually seem like real neighborhoods. When I visited the office, each hood was decorated to the hilt for Halloween. Sure, a lot of companies decorate, but EKS&H goes a step further. The children of the associates actually do their trick-or-treating in this building, and they come away with more candy and fun than they could in a week of canvassing their own neighborhoods back home. (It's much safer, too.)

The neighborhoods also instill a sense of competitive pride in their denizens—those who live (work) there. In addition to trying to outdo each other in the decoration department, the neighborhoods compete against each other during company outings and even during the workday in the form of pranks, which are legendary at EKS&H. (Remember the April Fool's Day Styrofoam packing peanuts?)

And it doesn't end there. EKS&H has a state-of-the-art workout facility, a break room retro-fitted like a '50s malt shop with complimentary soft drinks and snacks, and a *Harry Potter* room—a keypad-coded secure area exclusively for new mothers. There's a long list of reasons the company is recognized by its employees as the best place to work in the Denver area.

But it takes more than just great amenities to attract sharp young professionals and get them to go *all in* every single day.

Which is why the real story of EKS&H's success lies in its willingness to let Jim be Jim. Each neighborhood has its own manager, and it's the manager who's responsible—*encouraged* is probably the better word—for ensuring his or her team members have fun. For instance, if a manager suddenly decides to take her team out to happy hour at 3:00 PM, she can. The same goes for a team lunch or team bowling or what have you. There's no need to jump through management hoops to get a field trip approved. A simple email to the partners is all that's required, then out the door the team goes. As an EKS&H employee told me, "Whatever you feel you want to do, you have the freedom to do it."

Here, the boss is partially responsible for providing the fun, the break from monotony, for the employees. This attitude starts all the way at the top with the partners.

Goofing off is part of the office atmosphere as well. Pranks—filling your boss's car with packing peanuts or sticking a note on the cappuccino maker—are part of this freedom to enjoy yourself. There's a bit of reverse psychology going on here. Downtime is frowned upon in many offices, making it something forbidden and covert. Something enticing. After all, it's human nature to wonder just how much we can get away with.

When some downtime is allowed, it loses the fascination associated with rule-breaking and secrecy. It gains respect and is thus often shown respect by those who take advantage of it. Imagine, for instance, that your employees don't need to sneak out for a long lunch. They could instead simply tell their boss they're going to take a little extra time off. They wouldn't need to lie about having a doctor's appointment when they're really going to catch a ballgame. They would just tell their boss they're going to the game. More to the point, they wouldn't feel the need to have their fun only when the boss isn't looking.

It's this openness that allows EKS&H to have what Bob calls its "11-Month Work Year." As he explained it, "Some employees want to take some additional time off, like a month during the summer. We give people big blocks of time to do what they want because they give us big blocks of time."

Old School managers might recoil at the idea of such an office environment. They might assume that employees will surely abuse any such privileges given to them. Employees in an Old School atmosphere can't be trusted to make their own decisions. They can have the keys to the car only if they're carefully watched every second they're behind the wheel.

So why don't such abuses tend to happen at EKS&H? Why aren't employees always taking the afternoon off? Why don't they turn the 11-month work year into a 10-month work year (or 9 or 8...)?

Trust. It's embedded in the New School philosophy. It elevates employees from "bricks in the wall" to living, breathing people who can't sit at their desks for 10 straight hours or who might need a little more time at the beach or on the slopes. By granting employees so much freedom, EKS&H is saying, "If it's important to you, it's important to us. We trust you." The employees then return this trust with appreciation and a job well done.

Of course, as part of this trust-based relationship, employees also tend not to indulge in whatever fun activity their team or neighborhood has planned if there's pressing work to be done. As an employee at EKS&H said, "It's perfectly okay for our employees to miss planned events when there are clients to serve." Or if an upcoming company-wide event isn't a particular employee's cup of tea, the employee can bow out then too. And EKS&H is fine with that.

Ditch the Day-to-Day Routine

In the end, what does all this freedom at EKS&H mean? More focused employees for one thing. "There's not as much need to screw around during the day," said an employee. That makes sense because free time has been integrated into the workplace atmosphere. By turning free time into an asset, EKS&H continues to attract the best and the brightest accountants in the country. What's more, it keeps those talented people.

Bob and the rest of the EKS&H gang have also discovered another outlet for employee diversion. "We offer employees the opportunity to spend time in the community volunteering," Bob told me. "We pick a charity or charities each year to get our team together, and we bring massive labor to the effort. We come in and transform something, such as the Denver Children's Home or Habitat for Humanity. We build fences, do yard work. We take photos and frame them on what we call our Charity Wall." The employees' families are encouraged to participate as well. Volunteerism is an activity shared by the entire EKS&H community.

In our day-to-day lives, volunteer work often gets put on the back burner. There are only so many hours in the day. Yet if you've ever done volunteer work, then you know the sheer joy and sense of accomplishment that can come with it. That's the feeling that EKS&H makes sure its employees get out of its company-sponsored volunteer events.

Really, it's the same as giving employees an outlet for their penchant for fun. We all crave diversions from our day-in, day-out routines, and we seek out and find those diversions regardless of whether our bosses allow us to. Encouraging diversions—and breaks in the workday—is simply something that great companies do.

Holy Cow, What Now?

We started with an analogy that your atmosphere is like the planet Saturn. But don't for a second think that atmosphere is an intangible thing way out there in orbit, lacking identifiable form and substance. Instead, think of atmosphere as the end product of a carefully orchestrated seven-phase process. Think of it as your seven rings. Along those lines, effective "rings" don't just magically happen; they're deliberate.

That's not to say that your company will go without a workplace atmosphere unless you design and produce one. Every company has a workplace atmosphere, and if you and other leaders don't assume control of yours, your employees will. (Can you say "Dunder Mifflin"?)

I'd guess that your work history includes at least one experience where employee camaraderie was based on an openly shared dislike of the workplace atmosphere. I'd also guess that various aspects of that atmosphere (the rings) were ridiculed because they were obviously broken. Maybe there were few safety precautions, bullies roaming free, outdated equipment and uniforms, dim lighting, bad food choices in the company cafeteria, or broken vending machines. To put it another way, the atmosphere was a joke, and the owners, operators, and managers were the butt of that joke.

My first real leadership assignment was as the newly promoted general manager of a large health and fitness club in Colorado. One day, the owner pulled me aside and said, "Look, Eric, don't get too caught up in managing people and trying to bend them to your will. All you really need to do is to focus on creating the best atmosphere possible, one that allows each and every person on our payroll to feel a special connection to this club and to do their jobs to the very best of their abilities. If you do that and get out of the way, your people will make you look like a brilliant leader."

Let's just say that advice has stuck with me.

Igniters, Flamethrowers, and Burnout Extinguishers

1. **Distribute the Seven-Ring Assessment.** Survey your employees to get their responses to the *Seven-Ring Assessment* questions below. (The responses will be much more accurate if your employees are allowed to submit them anonymously.)

AGREE or DISAGREE?	Yes	No	Comments
My employer is doing everything possible to keep me safe at work.			
I can be my authentic self while I am work.			
I have everything I need to excel in this job (tools, equipment, technology, etc.).			
I like, respect, and trust my boss.			
I genuinely like the people I work with day in and day out.			
This environment energizes me and makes me want to perform.			
We have a fun, enjoyable workplace atmosphere.			

2. **Envision your ideal workplace.** Before you gather and review the responses above, complete this assessment as if you were an employee. How do you feel about your workplace atmosphere? What changes would you want made?

3. **Identify your office ambassadors**. Who are your office ambassadors? (For example, Judy is just one of many such ambassadors at EKS&H.) What do they love about your company? How many of your employees would say they would never want to leave such a great place? What are you doing to keep them?

4. **Give yourself a pat on the back**. Don't be too hard on yourself. Even if you've got a lot of work to do to create a better atmosphere, you're not exactly Six Companies. So list the various aspects of your culture that make your company a great place to work.

5. **Zap the norm**. If there were no restrictions or strict rules you had to abide by and you could redesign your entire workplace from scratch, what are the first things you would do? Would you consider putting in hammocks? Would your desk be similar to those that entry-level employees use? Would you create a special room where mothers could nurse their young children? Make a dream list and check a few items that you feel are within reason to try to accomplish.

Every company has a workplace atmosphere, and if you and other leaders don't assume control of yours, your employees will.

6. **Confront your fears**. What are you afraid will happen if you give employees too much freedom? (Come up with your worst-case scenarios here.) How does EKS&H counteract these risks? How might you counteract these risks?

7. **Make diversions deliberate**. What can you do intentionally in your workplace today, this week, and this year to break boredom and amuse your employees? The idea is to do something, anything that creates a bit of planned spontaneity and releases the tension.

8. **Let Jim be Jim**. Who are the "Jims" in your company? What ways can you think of to let Jim be Jim (especially when you're *not* running on a budget like that of the Googles of the world)? In what ways can you make your place of business more enjoyable even when the Jims you employ aren't necessarily working their dream jobs?

9. **Be a better boss**. Upgrading your atmosphere starts with U. In what ways can you be more compassionate, knowledgeable, accessible, fair, and supportive? Take an hour or two to think about this question and journal your responses. Then take a few minutes at the start of each day to review your notes and focus on making improvements in one or two areas that day.

10. **Break up the rigmarole**. How can you help employees counteract the more mundane aspects of work? How can you make your workplace atmosphere as enjoyable as possible so smart, talented people actually like being there and *choose* to work at your company over another?

Notes

1. Andrew Saunders, "Three Quarters Regret Career Choice, A Third Bored at Work Says Survey," *Management Today*, June 19, 2013, http://www.managementtoday.co.uk/news/1187016/three-quarters-regret-career-choice-third-bored-work-says-survey/.

2. Isabelle M. Bauer, "Coping with Life Regrets Across the Adult Lifespan," in *Reconstructing Emotional Spaces: From Experience to Regulation*, Prague College of Psychosocial Studies Press, 2011, http://www.pvsps.cz/data/document/20110715/9_Regret.pdf?id=687.

3. Rose Hoare, "Is Workplace Boredom 'the New Stress'?" CNN, May 2, 2012, http://edition.cnn.com/2012/05/02/business/workplace-boredom-stress/.

Chapter Five

GROWTH: Grow Them Big or They'll Go Home

In the summer of 2014, the biggest sports story was a rerun. The Miami Heat's LeBron James, fresh from a loss to the San Antonio Spurs in the Finals, was a free agent once again. The circumstances were nearly identical to four years earlier when LeBron, then with the Cleveland Cavaliers, had been a free agent and let it be known that he was on the market. One difference between 2014 and 2010 was the nationally televised press conference LeBron held to proclaim his decision back in 2010. In 2014, LeBron announced that he would return to Cleveland in *Sports Illustrated's* July 11 online addition. That day, 6.1 million unique visitors hit up the site to catch the details, breaking the site's record for single-day traffic.

However he chose to announce it, the motive behind both moves was largely the same: LeBron, the best player in the NBA, wanted to play for a championship team. His stint in Miami had proved quite successful in that regard. In four years, he had delivered two trophies to Miami fans. As LeBron himself said in his July 11, 2014 letter in *Sports Illustrated*, "When I left Cleveland, I was on a mission. I was seeking championships, and we won two. ...My goal is still to win as many titles as possible, no question. But what's most important for me is bringing one trophy back to Northeast Ohio."[1]

Before we go much further, let's be clear. LeBron's blatant opportunism has rubbed some fans the wrong way over the past few years. As a result, LeBron has dealt with his share of backlash. In July 2010, for example, Bryan Flynn in *The Bleacher Report* noted that LeBron "ripped the heart out of his home state [Ohio] and the team that drafted him." Not content to leave it there, Flynn went on to compare LeBron's allegedly shameful career choices against those of his forebears, noting, "Michael Jordan made the Chicago Bulls by winning six titles there, Larry Bird restored the Boston Celtics by winning three titles there, and Magic Johnson bought back the luster to Los Angeles winning five championships there."[2] Scores of sports reporters and countless fans had their own overwhelmingly negative words to describe their anger at what they deemed LeBron's betrayal.

I get it. I do. I remember the time when the Magic Johnsons and Larry Birds and Michael Jordans were loyal to their cities and their fans through thick and thin. Some of the world's greatest players stuck it out through loss after loss, spending their entire careers on mediocre or even terrible teams. While demonstrating such loyalty wasn't always ideal for the players' careers, we fans loved them for it. Such loyalty spoke of a certain purity and innocence, a devotion to the game, to their hometown, and to their devoted fans alike.

Then came the era of free agency, and everything changed. Nowadays, players hopscotch around the leagues like so many pieces on a checkerboard. Teams and the players initiate trades to improve their rosters—a double-edged sword for the fans who might still root for a losing team because of a particular player. As a result of free agency, players know to expect little loyalty from their teams. For their part, Old School fans have grown cynical, throwing their hands in the air and awaiting the day when their favorite power forward or quarterback or shortstop leaves in search of a bigger, better deal.

That's the reality. But LeBron's critics are still living in the past, which is why they attack LeBron for being so doggedly transparent in his pursuit of championship rings.

"Magic Johnson never did that!" they say.

"Larry Bird never did that!" they say.

"Michael Jordan never did that!"—well, at least not until he un-retired for a second time.

To which I say: Free agency is a game changer. Don't fight it. Accept it.

As it goes in professional sports, so it goes in the corporate world. There was a time when an employee and his or her employer were in it together for the long haul. Back then, people tended to spend their entire careers at a company, and that company returned its employees' loyalty with secure jobs, reasonable pay, and pensions. These days? Well, for starters, few companies can so much as guarantee a stable job with steady pay and benefits anymore. So if the companies can't offer loyalty, then why should they expect loyalty from their employees in turn?

Why indeed? And yet, many companies do demand loyalty, and the frustration of their leaders is almost palpable when employees don't toe the line.

Leaders who think this way are little different from LeBron's critics. They don't understand that employees won't give their loyalty unless they receive it first (and even then it's a gamble).

The reason why is simple. Because it's not really loyalty employees are after. What they really desire is a chance, a leg up. Another thing they want is mutuality. An employee who helps a company become successful expects to get a piece of the pie, a share of that success. It's like LeBron James on a quest for a ring. If he's going to *choose* to play for your team, then you had better put together a team with the potential to win it all. An employee might say it this way: "You get my labor, which helps you achieve your goals; I, in turn, get a shot at achieving my own goals." It's a two-way street.

Stop Fooling Yourself

We know that professional athletics changed because of free agency. So why did the workplace change? Without going into a long treatise on complex issues and trends, the short answer is that the economy has changed. On the corporate side, competition from abroad forced longstanding, entrenched U.S. firms to cut costs. They downsized, they shipped jobs overseas, and if all that failed they went out of business. Manufacturing, once a staple of the American economy, went abroad and will likely never return. Safe jobs, the kind that lasted for an entire career, were gone.

On the other end of the spectrum, the advent of the Internet, matched with cheap supply chains from foreign exporters, suddenly transformed a number of people sitting in front of their computers into instant entrepreneurs. Million-dollar companies sprang up overnight, then were gone the next day. Others—the Apples, Microsofts, Amazons, and Googles—survived, thrived, and transformed the U.S. economy. As the Old School model of employment withered, a New School model of innovation soared. In a sense, we've exchanged security for dynamic growth potential.

Though this analysis is admittedly hasty at best, the intent is to get you thinking about *why* employees today expect more. The curmudgeons among us chalk it up to entitlement. And while a sense of entitlement, particularly among the younger generations, surely plays a role, entitlement alone can't account for the fact that Americans today spend only about four years at any given job, according to the Bureau of Labor Statistics.[3] And this trend (if we can even call it that) goes back to the 1990s, clearly making it more than a generational issue where "kids" in the workplace supposedly kick back, relax, and expect the sun and the moon and the stars in exchange for little or nothing at all.

Entitlement or not, Old School managers have written off the possibility of loyalty from their employees, as if loyalty is some sort of Platonic ideal never to be realized in this dog-eat-dog world. "I've been giving Chandler a steady paycheck for the past two years, and today he had the nerve to hand me a resignation letter." That's what some managers are surely thinking. On the flip side, today's employees understand all too well that they're expendable assets. "I show up, I'm a productive member of my team, and I bust my behind working long hours to meet crazy deadlines. And what was I rewarded with? An email from HR; official notification that 'my services are no longer needed.'" That's what's running through some (soon-to-be-former) employees' minds.

That's the thing about real loyalty. It can't be bought. You won't get loyalty just because you give people a paycheck, no matter how many zeros are on it. Not when those people understand the nature of a competitive free market that comes with its share of layoffs, cutbacks, and buyouts. And not when those people are free agents who can move from team to team anytime they like.

> *You won't get loyalty just because you give people a paycheck, no matter how many zeros are on it.*

The larger problem, then, isn't that employees aren't loyal anymore; it's that managers have realized that buying loyalty doesn't work and have since given up on trying to instill loyalty in those employees. It's the age-old problem of cutting off your nose to spite your face. Giving up on producing loyal employees doesn't help anybody. It certainly doesn't help you, especially if you don't see the value in investing time and money in ungrateful people who are going to leave anyway. And it isn't helping the employees who, if they weren't looking for the exit before, are sure to start once they figure out that the company's goals and their own goals aren't even remotely in sync.

We're Here to Help You Grow, Even After You Go

When times are tough for the employees of Ben & Jerry's, they know the people at corporate headquarters won't turn their backs on them. And if worst comes to worst and employees have to be let go, it's not like an iron door slams behind them on their way out.

Ben & Jerry's culture is rooted in helping their employees through difficult transitions. When cutbacks are necessary or even when an employee is terminated, the company remains in contact with that employee throughout his or her transition to the next job. "Every person let go from Ben & Jerry's is reviewed by me and the board to determine their situation, their compensation, and their support mechanism," CEO Jostein Solheim told me. "Six months, one year, even three years later, we will check in with them to find out how they're doing, and if needed we'll help them in any way we can."

There's no law, regulation, or other obligation that forces a company to do anything once an employee is set free. But Ben & Jerry's employees know that the company cares for them as people, even when those employees are no longer on the payroll. Ben & Jerry's follow-up goes a whole lot further than most other companies. Noted Jostein, "It's not perfect, but when those realities kick in it's important that our people know we will follow it through all the way."

Helping people grow—even after they are no longer with you. Now that's a people-first culture!

What Do Your Employees Want?

There are limits to the extent an employer will go to keep an employee happy, even when the employee is a top performer or in one of those almost-impossible-to-replace positions. But unless they are feeling neglected, unappreciated, or mistreated, most employees would prefer not to go through a job change and would rather stay with their current employer, providing there exists a reasonable opportunity to learn and grow.

Deloitte released a benchmark study in 2011 titled "Talent Edge 2020: Building the Recovery Together: What Talent Expects and How Leaders Are Responding."[4] It should come as no surprise that the study shows that a majority of workers want to leave their jobs for better opportunities. In fact, only 35 percent expect to remain with their current employers—a 10-point decrease from 2009. As the study reveals, much of the difference is best explained by the improving economy. In 2009, in the face of recession, more workers were simply unwilling to test the job market and risk their current positions. But as the economy improved, so did workers' confidence that they could do better elsewhere.

For those employees looking to bolt, Deloitte found that a majority rated their current employers' "efforts at creating career paths, developing leaders, and retaining top performers" as fair or poor. Indeed, 53 percent looking to leave said that they would reconsider their decision if their current employers improved their job advancement and promotion prospects.

Let's take a moment to look at the other side of the coin. In a second Talent Edge 2020 survey of executives, 71 percent of respondents expressed a "high" or "very high" concern about retaining critical talent over the next 12 months, and 66 percent had the same concern about keeping high-potential talent. As noted in this second report, "Since companies can easily match compensation packages, Deloitte believes companies can differentiate themselves in the talent marketplace by going beyond financial incentives and creating customized retention strategies that address issues such as career advancement and greater recognition."[5]

Remember, fair compensation is the baseline—the starting point—for employees who are engaged and for those who go that extra step to become employees on fire. For the most part, throwing more cash at the problem isn't the solution. Giving employees the chance to show their stuff, build stronger skills, and grow at the company—this is the solution, or at least an essential part of the solution.

It's impossible to overstate the importance today's employees place on training, growth, and opportunities to advance. Where the first Deloitte study really stands apart is that it found that a majority of workers would stay if they believed they had a future at their current firm/organization, a future that requires more from them and can bestow more riches upon them. It also shows that if their current employer can provide those opportunities, employees won't seek opportunities elsewhere.

The two important takeaways from the Deloitte study?

1. Your people want—actually demand—opportunities to grow and fulfill their potential.

2. Finding a new job is a hassle, and, all else being equal, employees will stay if they believe their manager will help them grow at the company.

The more skilled and talented employees are, the more likely they are to be motivated to learn new skills, develop their talents and expertise, and improve their perceived value both at your company and in the marketplace. Any top performer who works for you wants to be better tomorrow than they are today. Moreover, those top performers may even be imagining the day when they themselves are in your job or at a similar level within your organization or somewhere else. And that's a good thing. Such ambition should be acknowledged and applauded because it means they're thirsty for more and are driven to excel and grow. When you recognize ambition in your people, the objective should be clear: Make sure you're as motivated as they are so you can help them reach their potential. That's when you'll capture their hearts and souls. As the research shows, most of those who are secretly looking to leave would actually prefer to stay—*as long as you give them a compelling reason to do just that.*

If you're looking to build a workforce that's on fire, then part of your job is to give them a reason to be on fire.

Cross Training for Career Gaining

I could hear the pride in Bill Marriott's voice. "Fifty percent of our general managers started out as hourly workers," he told me. Talk about employee growth! Indeed, when I spoke with Bill he went out of his way to tell me about the growth potential for Marriott employees. If condensed to a rule, the Marriott Method would be this: Any employee can perform in several other capacities at a moment's notice.

That's on account of the training Marriott provides. New and even long-time employees are constantly trained to know the ins and outs of every essential job in any Marriott hotel. "No one learns just one job," Bill said. "We cross-train everyone to the point where a front desk person can also work in a restaurant, run the gift shop, or dish up a banquet. If business is slow in one area, employees can be useful in another." That way, anyone can help out whenever a guest needs it.

This philosophy—that no job is too large or too small for any Marriott employee—is essential for a profitable hotel chain. You can't always guarantee that the right person with the right training will be right where you need him or her at any given moment. What you can usually guarantee, however, is that someone is around. Which is why that someone had better able to step up to the task.

The result is not only an exceptionally well-run hotel chain but also a workforce that stays. "Our average GM has been in their position for 25 years," Bill told me. "And we have the lowest churn [turnover rate] in the industry."

Marriott also makes a point of hiring people for their personal strengths. As Bill noted, "We hire friendly and train technical." In other words, the key characteristic for hotel employees is how personable they are. Marriott isn't as concerned about whether an applicant already knows how to make hotel reservations because those skills can be taught. "An applicant's attitude and desire to serve others— that's what determines whether or not we'll ask them to come work for us," said Bill.

Loud Growth at the Quiet Company

"Work 12-hour days, hit the phones, don't let the rejection get to you, and work as hard as possible while you're young...and someday off in the not-too-distant future, you will have a solid client base and flexibility in your career."

That's the underlying promise many large insurance and financial securities companies make to the eager young college grads they attempt to recruit as sales associates. Those who accept the challenge are on-boarded through an intense training program to learn the business and the tricks of the trade. Then, after a young sales associate burns through their list of friends and family members, they must find new prospects by cold-calling people they've never met. No wonder the attrition rate for young sales associates in this industry is off the charts.

With sales offices throughout the country, Northwestern Mutual has been a staple of the U.S. insurance industry for more than 157 years. Once known as "the quiet company," they made a lot of noise in 2013 by posting revenues in excess of $23 billion. That same year, the company received the Employees' Choice Award by Glassdoor.com, an online career and workplace community.[6] Given that Glassdoor uses anonymous employee surveys to rank its best places to work, such honors come with the kind of genuine legitimacy sometimes lacking from other awards. To top it off, Northwestern Mutual was the only company in the insurance industry to rank in the top 50 of Glassdoor's Best Places to Work in 2013. There's obviously something very special about the way Northwestern Mutual engages its people.

Which brings us to the story of Monica. Monica began her career as a receptionist at one of Northwestern Mutual's local sales offices in Colorado. While happy in her job, Monica hoped to challenge herself further and receive more complex job responsibilities. But before she could grow out of her current position, she knew she first had to begin with a solid foundation and master the tasks associated with keeping the office running.

It wasn't long before Scott Theodore, who oversaw that office, noticed how well Monica performed. In fact, she was so good that he promoted her to be his executive assistant. It was a natural progression for Monica, who was ecstatic at the opportunity.

Monica responded with her usual gung-ho enthusiasm. She invested time and energy in learning everything she could, earned the appropriate licensing, and built great relationships with Scott's clients. Unfortunately, the administrative part of this job was not her "sweet spot." After almost a year, Scott realized that this particular job wasn't the best fit for Monica's talents. Monica recognized it too. At this point, most firms would have either let Monica go or demoted her back to the role of receptionist.

As the research shows, most of those who are secretly looking to leave would actually prefer to stay—as long as you give them a compelling reason to do just that.

Scott had a better idea.

Rather than return her to the receptionist role, Scott decided to make the most of Monica's great energy and relationship skills and put her in charge of recruiting for the office. In Scott's words, that's when Monica "caught fire." She was a natural recruiter—personable, connected, organized, and diligent. Because Monica had worked at the Northwestern Mutual-Denver office for some time, she knew exactly the type of person who fit in best with the culture. Scott became a managing partner of Northwestern Mutual-Denver soon after and eventually promoted Monica to the role of Recruiting Officer, the individual responsible for building the firm's sales force.

But the story doesn't end there. After a few successful years, it became clear to Scott and the rest of the team that Monica had higher aspirations. When he asked her if she had any further goals in mind, she told Scott that she would love to start her own consulting firm.

Whoa. Wait a minute. When Scott asked Monica about her goals, surely he meant her goals *at Northwestern Mutual*, right? Surely he didn't anticipate that she would express a desire to leave. What had happened was this: Scott had given Monica so many opportunities and had trained her so well that her ambition and confidence grew as a result. And therein lies the danger of growing your own talent. You train them and train them, then train them some more, and what do they do? They scoop up that training and take off running toward the next best thing.

Yet Scott didn't see it that way. In fact, he and Northwestern Mutual helped Monica get her new venture off the ground. Before too long, Monica wasn't just serving one Northwestern Mutual office; instead, she branched out and began serving the recruiting needs of twelve other managing partners at Northwestern Mutual offices throughout the nation.

As Scott said, "I didn't see it as losing a great employee. I saw it as twelve of my colleagues gaining a great asset." These days, Scott surmises, ten percent of Monica's recruiting work is on behalf of Northwestern Mutual-Denver; the rest of the time she serves other Northwestern Mutual clients across the country.

Monica's story showcases how an employer and an employee can work together to help each other and raise each other's game. Monica was promoted as a means of recognizing her good work and helping the firm achieve or even exceed its recruitment goals. Her promotion strengthened the firm's recruitment efforts, as did encouraging her to realize her dream and go off on her own. The story also demonstrates how a leader truly paid attention to the personal strengths of his employees. After all, there is a plethora of other financial services firms that wouldn't have bothered with the receptionist's career goals, instead focusing their time on growing the people who matter most to their own interests.

Scott recognized that Monica was an essential part of Northwestern Mutual's success from her time as a receptionist onward.

And as it turns out, Monica isn't alone in being on the receiving end of the company's commitment to growing talent. Scott Theodore himself has experienced those benefits firsthand.

"This is the last place I thought I'd be working," Scott told me. With a degree in petroleum engineering and geology, Scott began his career as an engineer. But after a quirk of fate left Scott unemployed, he turned to some friends who happened to work at Northwestern Mutual. Not long thereafter, he started as a financial representative, and today he runs Northwestern Mutual-Denver, which has 125 financial representative and advisors and 30 employees.

What explains Scott's complete career change? "Opportunity for growth and a career with impact and purpose," he said simply. "Twenty-six years ago, I left the professional world of engineering, and now I'm a managing partner at Northwestern Mutual." He shook his head and laughed, almost as if he couldn't quite believe it either.

"When we recruit people, we talk about career development right from the start," Scott said. He also explained that there are two paths open for new representatives—personal financial management and leadership. You see, Scott wants to know where his new recruits' heads are at before they even start the job. "We're not just looking with a mindset that we want someone to fill a particular role. We want someone with the capacity to expand and evolve into the path that's right for them," he said.

When the individual is given opportunities to reach his or her full potential, the firm prospers. When the individual is expected to play a specific role that meets only the needs of the firm, the individual's growth is limited. It's like tossing a bucket of water on the passion the individual has for the job and for the employer. It's a lose/lose scenario.

Building, Connecting, and Growing at the Boston Consulting Group

Ranked #3 on *Fortune*'s 100 Best Places to Work in 2014 and #2 on Glassdoor.com's *25 Best Companies To Work For If You Want To Get Promoted Fast*, the Boston Consulting Group knows the importance career growth plays in finding and keeping top talent in their highly competitive industry. Leveraging the first letters of their company name, Boston Consulting Group brands itself to prospective employees as Build Connect Grow. Their employment website (http://careers.bcg.com) allows prospective job candidates to do far more than apply for jobs—it provides them with a snapshot of four potential career paths—scientist, engineer, expert, and strategist. From there, candidates can see how they would fit in with the company culture, learn about the specific kinds of opportunities that lie ahead, and read quotes and reviews from other company professionals who've followed these four career paths.

Make Progress toward Goals

Each new financial representative at Northwestern Mutual also gets a mentor. The mentor's job, according to Scott, is to make sure the new representative's questions are answered. "We also want the mentor to make sure the new representatives are achieving their goals so they can further their vision," he said.

As was the case with Monica, Northwestern Mutual-Denver has no qualms about helping both their employees and representatives grow in their roles. The company helps with licensing and supports them throughout the process.

Northwestern Mutual boasts one of the lowest turnover rates in the industry. And it all starts with the company's acknowledgment that their financial representatives have long-term dreams they want to fulfill.

It's a lesson Scott has never forgotten. "I see myself as the keeper of the culture," he tells me. "From my perspective, my role as managing partner is to help people figure out what their natural talents are and challenge them to use those talents with the ultimate goal of calling out greatness."

The result of this above-and-beyond commitment to growth? Northwestern Mutual's talent is the envy of the industry.

The Growth-Retention Index

It doesn't take a Harvard research study or a Gallup poll survey to make a strong argument that employees who are learning new skills, mastering their existing skills, and gaining more experience in a variety of areas are more inclined to stay with their employers than those who feel unchallenged and bored. (All of which, of course, is contingent upon their feeling that their compensation, recognition, and rewards are in alignment with the value they bring to the table.) Simultaneously, as employees increase the value they bring to their employers, it's no secret that their employers should be increasing their compensation, responsibilities, and opportunities commensurately.

It's not exactly rocket science, right?

So long as there's growth on both sides of the equation, harmony exists and balance reigns. However, a disconnect occurs when either or both parties feel as if they're getting the raw end of the deal—giving more than they're getting.

Employee growth and employer retention are tightly linked. When diagrammed, it might look something like this:

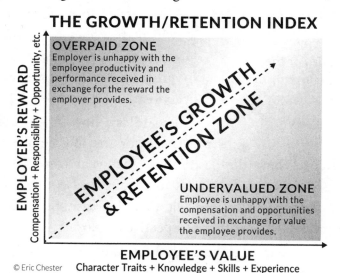

THE GROWTH/RETENTION INDEX

OVERPAID ZONE
Employer is unhappy with the employee productivity and performance received in exchange for the reward the employer provides.

EMPLOYEE'S GROWTH & RETENTION ZONE

UNDERVALUED ZONE
Employee is unhappy with the compensation and opportunities received in exchange for value the employee provides.

EMPLOYER'S REWARD
Compensation + Responsibility + Opportunity, etc.

EMPLOYEE'S VALUE
Character Traits + Knowledge + Skills + Experience

© Eric Chester

The Overpaid Zone—No employer can remain competitive if they consistently pay higher wages than an employee's productivity and performance merit. Thus, big problems come in when high compensation and increased responsibility and autonomy are given to an employee who doesn't have the skills and abilities to match. The result is a shortened lifespan of the employment contract.

The Undervalued Zone—Employees who consistently improve their job-related knowledge, experience, and skill set deserve increased compensation and responsibility. Employers who fail to recognize these improvements or adjust pay and responsibility levels accordingly are at high risk of losing valuable contributors.

Five-Step Process for Staying in the Growth and Retention Zone

Some employees are hired because they possess a skill set that's in demand. The software developers an engineering firm hires have experience coding, just as the chefs a restaurant hires know their way around an industrial kitchen. Unskilled employees are brought in to an organization because they have demonstrated the aptitude and the desire to acquire the skills needed to perform the job for which they have been hired, either through the company's training program or through some sort of apprenticeship on-the-job learning.

So long as there's growth on both sides of the equation, harmony exists and balance reigns.

Regardless how they obtain the skills they need for the job, employees worth their paycheck have the desire to get better at what they do. Furthermore, most employees want to acquire and develop new skills, talents, and abilities that will help them increase their value to their present employers and other prospective employers.

To ignore your employees' need for continual skills development is akin to ignoring your garden's need for frequent watering; the seeds you've planted are not going to grow, and your existing flowers are going to wilt.

It's simple really. You want them to grow, and they want to grow. So let's focus attention on a five-step how-to formula to ensure your employees remain in the growth and retention zone, which leads to long-time on-fire performance.

1. **Agree on a growth agenda**. One reason couples often cite for a failed marriage is that the husband and wife discovered over time that they each wanted different things that couldn't both exist in a shared life. For example, the bride dreamed of moving to a small house in the country and raising a few children while the groom has no interest in parenthood and likes living a fast-paced lifestyle in a downtown high-rise. No matter how much they love each other, one or the other is not going to get what they really want, and their future together is tenuous. The employment relationship works the same way—both parties have to be moving in the same direction. This sort of mutuality requires both parties to meet at the onset of the hire, as well as periodically discuss, agree to, and map out each of their future ambitions. It also requires the same kind of two-way trust and transparency that was evident in the working relationship between Scott and Monica at Northwestern Mutual.

2. **Establish the timetable**. Just as both parties need to agree on what new skills and abilities the employee is going to be learning, they also need to establish and agree upon the time frame. Without a timetable in place, one or both parties are going to eventually disengage. Something like this: "Here's where you are now. To get where you want to be, you're going to need to acquire certifications A and B and gain experience

doing C. This process typically takes three years, but we can cut some of that time off if you enroll in the classes for certification A next month."

3. **Individualize the learning methodology**. As a former high school teacher, I can attest to the importance of figuring out how each student learns best. Hand some people a textbook and they've got it, while others require a lesson and Q&A. Others need a visual demonstration or a lab to grasp the concepts. Knowing how each employee learns and designing the learning agenda around what works best for them are the keys to ensuring that they stay on course.

4. **Celebrate milestones and success**. Many of us can recall when our parents charted our height on a doorway. They'd mark our height, and when we stepped back we could see how much taller we had grown since the last time they measured us. Even a half-inch of progress drew applause and cheers. Then if you had a father like mine, you were told that you'd grow even faster if you ate your vegetables and went to bed on time. Again, the same principles are at work here. It's important to chart the growth progress of each employee and let them recognize how much they're learning, how much experience they're gaining, and how much more valued they are becoming to you in the process. The more significant the milestone (e.g., degrees earned or newly acquired certifications), the larger the celebration should be (e.g., office celebration with cake, article of congratulations in the company grapevine, or taking the employee and his or her spouse out for dinner).

5. **Rinse and repeat**. The old adage "You're either green and growing or you're ripe and rotten" is one that's

very much at play in your culture. Every employee, from your receptionist to your EVP, needs to be on a growth trajectory—and they need to understand and agree on that growth trajectory. Once they get where they want to be, they're going to see a new future for themselves off in the horizon. That's a good thing for them and for your organization.

On Fire in the Kitchen Means Big Business

Every time I'm in southern Florida, I make a beeline for Pollo Tropical, a chain of fast casual restaurants throughout the Deep South that specializes in char-grilled chicken served Caribbean style. Although the food is amazing, it's the frontline service that impresses me most.

The recipe for success at Pollo Tropical begins with employee retention. In fact, the average employee tenure in their core market of Miami is more than three years. You're probably thinking the same thing I thought: *"Who works in the same fast-food job for six years?"* Just to be clear, that's the retention rate for all employees, not just upper management.

While competitors in the fast casual restaurant industry confront turnover rates for managers of 80 percent or higher, the turnover rate for Pollo Tropical's managers is less than 25 percent. Just pop into any one of Pollo's 125 locations, and the odds are better than 40 percent that the general manager has been with Pollo for eight years or longer. That's as rare in the restaurant industry as an alligator sighting in Alaska.

To understand how this phenomenon occurs, I caught up with Vicky Timmer, VP of Operations, who has more than 20 years of experience with the brand. She first gave me some statistics that she felt would help me better comprehend their remarkable culture. At least half of the managers of Pollo Tropical restaurants were born outside of the United States, and about 70 percent of them speak English as their second language. She then began to share stores about the people behind those metrics.

Vicky told me about Silvia, a single mother who came to the US from Honduras 17 years ago and has worked at Pollo Tropical ever since. Silvia learned English during her time as a line server at Pollo, then worked her way up to cashier, team leader, and manager. After spending years improving her language and management skills through Pollo's internal development programs, she was promoted to general manager. She now runs one of the company's highest-volume restaurants. In the meantime, her daughter has grown up, graduated from college, and was accepted into medical school at a Florida university on a 100 percent scholarship.

She talked about Oscar, who came to the US on a raft from Cuba with just $50 in his pocket. His first job was for Pollo Tropical, where he worked for years in various positions before advancing to the position of general manager. At the 15-year mark, Oscar left Pollo to take a job with a competitor that offered him more money and benefits. After four months, Oscar came back to Pollo because his employer didn't really care about their people or their customers. He said working there was "just a job," but working at Pollo was like working with family.

She then shared stories about two other managers. Colombian-born Carlos started as a griller, learned English, and steadily moved up the ladder to become a manager and eventually a district manager. His daughter has since graduated from college and works as a graphic artist, and his son is attending medical school. Joseph, in turn, came to the U.S. from Ghana. He has a degree in HR and speaks six languages, and he worked his way up to district manager. In 2006, he was named District Manager of the Year. His success enabled him and his wife to buy their first home in 2008.

Vicky could have shared stories for hours on end about people who came to Pollo with little more than a desire to work and a dream of a better life. Pollo's culture is such that it arms the people they hire with both opportunities and the tools they need to make those dreams come true.

What Pollo Tropical gets in return are people who seek and achieve continual professional growth and who stick around for the long haul—people who are *on fire at work*.

 ## Igniters, Flamethrowers, and Burnout Extinguishers

As mentioned earlier, "Deloitte believes companies can differentiate themselves in the talent marketplace by going beyond financial incentives and creating customized retention strategies that address issues such as career advancement and greater recognition." With that thought in mind, let's spend a few minutes looking at how you're differentiating yourself in the marketplace. Here are some questions to ask yourself:

1. What's the turnover rate at your company? Is that rate higher than average for your industry? Is it higher than you would like it to be?

2. Deloitte noted that "employees who describe their companies' talent programs as 'world-class' or 'very good' are nearly twice (42 percent to 23 percent) as committed to remaining at their jobs than employees who work at companies with 'fair' or 'poor' talent efforts." How would you describe your company's talent programs? How do you think your employees would describe them?

   To ignore your employees' need for continual skills development is akin to ignoring your garden's need for frequent watering; the seeds you've planted are not going to grow, and your existing flowers are going to wilt.

3. What's your personal take on LeBron James? Opportunist? Trailblazer? Narcissist? Someone who knows his own mind and goes after what he wants?

4. How many of your employees' career goals do you know? What do each of your employees see as his or her championship ring?

5. Once you know your employees' goals, what specifically do you do to help them achieve those goals? What more can you do?

6. In your annual, midyear, and/or periodic employee reviews, do you spend time talking about and mapping

out your employees' career goals? Do the plans written on the page or discussed in your meetings align with real-world plans for growth and advancement? If not, what specifically are you willing to do to revamp that review process?

7. To what degree do you "hire friendly and train technical" the way that Marriott does? To what degree does such a hiring policy seem to make sense for your organization?

8. Scott Theodore at Northwestern Mutual noted, "We're not just looking with a mindset that we want someone to fill a particular role. We want someone with the capacity to expand and evolve into the path that's right for them." Think of Monica's job progression from receptionist to executive assistant to recruiter to director of recruiting to owner of her own recruiting firm. Why did Northwestern Mutual take such a strong interest in her career growth? In what ways did the company benefit from her continual career development?

9. Think back to Vicky Timmer's stories of Silvia, Oscar, Carlos, and Joseph at Pollo Tropical. In what ways do those stories demonstrate how on-fire commitment to your people leads to their on-fire commitment to you? How many of your employees' stories can you tell?

10. Do you ask employees about their job goals again after you hire them? What gets them out of bed in the morning? What do they love doing? What kinds of things do they want to learn? How willing are you to open the door so motivated employees can decide whether or not they want to walk through it?

Notes

1. LeBron James as told to Lee Jenkins, "LeBron: I'm Coming Back to Cleveland," *Sports Illustrated*, July 11, 2014, http://www.si.com/nba/2014/07/11/lebron-james-cleveland-cavaliers.

2. Bryan Flynn, "LeBron James Chooses Miami, Now the Anti-LeBron Backlash Begins," *Bleacher Report*, July 8, 2010, http://bleacherreport.com/articles/417603-lebron-james-choses-miami-now-the-anti-lebron-backlash-begins.

3. Employee Tenure News Release, U.S. Department of Labor, Bureau of Labor Statistics, September 18, 2012, http://www.bls.gov/news.release/archives/tenure_09182012.htm.

4. "Talent Edge 2020: Building the Recovery Together—What Talent Expects and How Leaders Are Responding," Deloitte, April 2011, https://www.deloitte.com/assets/Dcom-Poland/Local%20Assets/Documents/Raporty,%20badania,%20rankingi/pl_TalentEdge2020_Recovery.pdf.

5. "Talent Edge 2020: Redrafting Talent Strategies for the Uneven Recovery," Deloitte, January 2012, http://www.deloitte.com/assets/Dcom-UnitedStates/Local%20Assets/Documents/IMOs/Talent/US_TalentEdge2020January2012_010612.pdf.

6. Press Release, "Northwestern Mutual Honored as One of Top 50 Best Places to Work in 2013 [by Glassdoor.com]," Northwestern Mutual, http://www.northwesternmutual.com/learning-center/article-library/glassdoor-award.aspx.

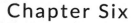

Chapter Six

ACKNOWLEDGEMENT:
What It Really Means to Put Your People First

"I love it. I love going to work every day. I love the people I work with. It's just such a positive and great environment. I love it."

"It makes me smile, makes me know that I'm doing something awesome, that I'm treating my customers with so much respect, which is great for me."

These comments—and many more like them—came from engaged, on-fire employees who work for a company that has made *Fortune*'s "100 Best Places to Work For" every year since the list began in 1998. In fact, it's one of just 13 companies to hold this special distinction, which is why *Fortune* decided to include them on an even more exclusive list, its "Best Companies All Stars."[1]

So it might come as a surprise to learn that the company in question is a grocery store chain. But not just any grocery store. We're talking about Wegmans Food Markets. In fact, in 2012 and 2014 Consumer Reports named Wegmans the best supermarket chain in the United States.[2] Yeah, it's that good.

A few years ago, I had the privilege of speaking for several hundred of Wegmans' managers. To prepare for that assignment, I asked Gerry Pierce, SVP of Human Resources, if I could first interview some of the frontline workers to get a better idea of some of the challenges the managers might be facing. Now, most companies would balk at this kind of request. Or funnel you through the PR department, where you'd find yourself talking to a spokesperson skilled at delivering the corporate sales pitch to position them in the best possible light. Even those companies that wouldn't balk at such a request would likely bristle at the idea of letting an outsider walk into their offices or stores and start asking questions.

But not Wegmans. Gerry Pierce was happy to oblige.

"Sure," came the immediate response to my inquiry. "Just let the manager know you're there, and you can talk to anyone you like."

Seriously? Anyone? Even if I bring a video camera?

"No problem."

So that's exactly what I did. I walked up and down the aisles of the Wegmans in Rochester, New York, asking questions of random employees. I recorded their answers, two of which I quoted above. (By the way, I should probably mention that those comments came from teenage employees. I purposely interviewed only teens stocking shelves, sweeping floors, taking out the trash, and sacking groceries. We're talking about employees paid at or just slightly above minimum wage. You know, the kinds of employees who are regularly maligned for being entitled, lazy, disengaged, and unable to carry on a face-to-face conversation with an adult.)

Here's what happened in a nutshell: Across the board, the Wegmans employees I talked to couldn't have been happier to tell me, a perfect stranger, exactly how much they enjoyed being part of the team. Their enthusiasm was infectious almost to the point of elation. I started to think I should apply for a job. Or that maybe they had somehow managed to "stack the deck" and bring in a group of trained young actors to play a part. Of course, that wasn't the case.

That's when it hit me. Wegmans' corporate brass was so amenable to my request because they knew what I'd find. Total confidence in your workforce tends to breed that type of bravado. Think about it—most other companies would have fired the poor guy who green-lit a request to record for all eternity what their employees *really thought*.

Not Wegmans. Their corporate leaders *know* how their people feel about their job, their colleagues, and their customers. They were brimming with...well, love. It's no wonder that Wegmans has turnover that's less than half of the industry average.[3]

People who go to work for Wegmans may initially arrive with a "just another job" mindset, but it doesn't take long until most realize they've found a career and never want to leave.

Acknowledgement Trumps Recognition

What company wouldn't kill to have this degree of loyalty? Wegmans must be offering some serious compensation and benefit packages to foster such a devoted workforce. At least that's what I figured. Yet according to *Fortune*, Wegmans pretty much pays equal to or better than the competition, without leading the market. The company manages to be the employer-of-choice in grocery retailing by taking a holistic view of Total Rewards, one that embraces all aspects of the employee experience without having to offer pay for sabbaticals, childcare, or 100 percent of healthcare.

What is it then that sets them apart?

In a word, Wegmans *acknowledges* its employees. It's engrained in their culture as deeply as it's engrained into Maslow's hierarchy of needs. In a world where everyone wants to feel like they belong and that they matter, Wegmans is the high-water mark for employee acknowledgement.

Notice I didn't say *recognition*. That's because acknowledgement is really a higher order of recognition. To acknowledge something requires thought plus action, whereas to recognize something is often a neutral, passive act. You *recognize* the distinctive human forms in a Picasso painting. You *acknowledge* the painting's beauty and the artist's mastery.

That's not to say recognition isn't important. It's no secret that employees crave recognition. In Globoforce's 2013 employee "Mood Tracker" survey, 94 percent of employees said they like getting recognized for accomplishments at work. Similarly, 82 percent said that getting recognized for efforts at work motivates them in their jobs.[4] Employees want to be seen. They want their employers to know they exist.

Far too many companies, however, treat recognition as just another form of compensation. However, compensation and benefits are negotiated terms, mutually agreed upon, expected at regular intervals, and in many cases legally enforced. In other words, they're *expected*. We already talked a bit about how to beat an employee's compensation expectations, but many organizations behave as if the only ways to recognize their people are to provide compensation and benefits and to deal with recognition at periodic intervals like during performance reviews and ceremonial award dinners.

At its most basic level, the Old School idea of recognition is that you get a paycheck at the end of the day. Anything over and above that check is a bonus reserved for extraordinary service or contribution. However, this plan leaves those employees who meet expectations with little or nothing above their paycheck feeling, as Pink Floyd famously sang back in the '80s, as if they're "just another brick in the wall."

No one wants to be just another brick...a number...an expendable resource. For the 21,000 workers tasked with building the Hoover Dam in the midst of the Great Depression, that was just the way things were, and you had better keep shoveling or your job would go to the next man. However, in today's world letting employees at any level feel like they're just another brick in your wall is a surefire way to completely disenfranchise your workforce and accelerate your turnover.

Recognition is no longer enough.

Recognition by itself doesn't carry enough force or mean very much, which is likely why so many employers fall back on Old School incentive programs.

But most incentive programs don't really recognize much of anything. For one, incenting someone to do something is like a bribe: I will give you a treat, but only if you finish your Brussels sprouts. You've already told your employees exactly what needs to be done in order to receive a reward, so they know what's coming or at least are expecting something for their efforts. The recognition in this case is actually a form of compensation.

With rare exceptions, incentive programs are just that—programs. Everyone is treated the same. Every action is treated the same. You're just another brick, only this time you're a brick with a bonus. Worse, you're just a brick incentivized to perform a certain task. If your incentive program doles out $50 for every $10,000 in sales, what about the salesperson who hits $9,999? She was one dollar away from getting a reward. Too bad. Rules are rules. And yet she still brought in $9,999. Is she supposed to feel recognized?

> *With rare exceptions, incentive programs are just that— programs. Everyone is treated the same. Every action is treated the same. You're just another brick, only this time you're a brick with a bonus.*

It's steak knives all over again. First place, Cadillac El Dorado. Second place, steak knives. Third, well, you know…. There's only one winner in this scheme, and it's the lucky SOB who wins the Caddy.

If all employers have are rigid programs or contests, then they're missing most of what it means to recognize an employee. Because acknowledgement isn't a program. It can't be automated, nor can it be impersonal. It requires caring, personalization, and a human touch.

Recognition 101

In my book *Getting Them to Give a Damn*, I outlined my Four Ps of Recognition and Reward. They are:

1. *Personal*: Regardless of the type of recognition, its perceived value escalates when it's individualized for the employee.

2. *Proportionate and Pertinent*: Any recognition or reward should always match the level of performance being recognized and should always correlate directly with the employee's actions.

3. *Prompt*: Celebrating an employee's "above and beyond" actions the moment you see them is far more effective than patting the employee on the back six months later during the performance review.

4. *Public*: The value of a reward multiplies exponentially in the presence of peers and colleagues.

Wegmans doesn't confine itself to a passive, rote recognition program like those used by so many organizations. Instead, they subscribe to a different philosophy.

We need to acknowledge all of our people on a regular basis.

Employees First, Customers Second

The title of this section is Wegmans' credo—and it's also a play on the Number 1 rule in business, which is that the customer always comes first. Wegmans' success suggests that the Number 1 rule is Old School. The New School puts employees first.

With 86 stores in six states, 44,000 employees, and annual revenue of roughly $7 billion, Rochester-based Wegmans is by no means small potatoes. But outside the northeast and mid-Atlantic region, not a lot of consumers have ever heard of Wegmans. The company is privately owned by the Wegmans family, and this is exactly the way the company wants it. Its growth has been deliberate rather than explosive. But believe me, if you've ever been inside a Wegmans, it's an experience you'll never forget. Walking into a Wegmans is like walking into a research lab for food. The employees in each department are extremely well trained and, if needed, can speak intelligently for hours about the items in their respective departments. When I was glancing at some expensive cheeses in the dairy department, one of the associates guided me over to the cracker aisles and pointed out one brand that she promised would make the cheese an "investment" I wouldn't forget. She told me the color of the cow in Brazil that produced the milk and why no other milk would suffice. Her passion and enthusiasm were extremely rare among retail employees and even more rare in a supermarket. However, that kind of passion and enthusiasm was very common in the associates I met in every aisle of Wegmans.

> Acknowledgement isn't a program. It can't be automated, nor can it be impersonal. It requires caring, personalization, and a human touch.

What's even more remarkable is that no employee at Wegmans has ever been laid off. When Wegmans eliminates a position, it finds a new job for the displaced employee in another store or division. In fact, when the company closed one of its Rochester stores, it sent all 250 employees to work at another store in the city. That's living your credo.

Of course, not every business can avoid layoffs. Nor do I want to give the impression that layoffs are always bad. But the story is indicative of the culture at Wegmans—a culture that always puts employees first.

Let's take a moment to dig a bit deeper into this culture. It's all well and good to be lauded by the media, but awards and positive press don't show how the culture came about; instead, they simply reward the result.

Lead by Example

There's no "Be Nice to Employees" chapter in the Wegmans manager guidebook. At Wegmans, "lead by example" is no cliché as new hires are engrained with a cultural credo that they begin to model from day one. They actively demonstrate what it means to acknowledge their coworkers. By the time an employee makes store manager, that employee has been promoted many times and continually acknowledged for the way he or she acknowledges others.

Sound redundant? It is. That's how acknowledgement becomes inculcated throughout an entire culture. It's like a nonstop audio track being played the moment every employee sets foot into a Wegmans: *"We see you. We're happy you're here. You're important to us. We're a cut above, and because you're one of us you're a cut above. Let's do this together!"*

It's so tightly woven into the Wegmans culture that it's become self-replicating. Managers walk the talk by showcasing the Wegmans' credo to new hires who learn the same invaluable lesson: To advance, I must act like my manager, support my teammates, and spread encouragement.

Those who don't get it don't advance and likely don't survive in their jobs.

CARE

It's not as if Wegmans leaves employee acknowledgement totally up to chance. They have a more formal recognition program called CARE—Caring, Appreciation, and Recognizing Each Other—that follows my Four Ps of Recognition and Reward almost to the letter. The rules of the program state that an employee (any employee—it doesn't have to be a supervisor or manager) can acknowledge any other employee for work above and beyond. Pertinent and prompt? Check. The nominated employee receives a CARE card telling them who nominated them and for what reason. Personal and public? Check. The CARE cards are handed out in front of the other store employees, and the employee's actions are shared on the company-wide intranet. As for proportionate, CARE cards usually come with a free meal, though the meal seems like mere window dressing. The proportionate element really comes from the acknowledgement of colleagues—both in store and across this remarkable company—who know that the employee is working the Wegmans way.

Wegmans also rewards good customer service with three different tiers of acknowledgement. When a customer informs Wegmans (via the manager, email, etc.) about an employee's exceptional service, the company recognizes that employee and makes sure the entire company knows about it. The highest tier, known as the Superstar Award, comes with a personal letter from the senior VP of consumer affairs and an in-store ceremony, where colleagues are on hand to witness the manager pin the Superstar award to the employee's jacket.

From the moment they punch in, Wegmans employees experience a culture that has been built around acknowledging them as critically important to the company's success.

Finally, as is quite typical in business, Wegmans has appreciation days for its employees. Ho-hum, right? Not exactly. At Wegmans, each store has complete autonomy to conduct its employee appreciation days as it sees fit. In practice, the store manager and those employees on the store CARE team decide amongst themselves how the store will show appreciation for its employees. And each store puts up the money for its own appreciation days, an investment that feeds back into the company culture. Employees know that the manager isn't playing with some corporate piggy bank. Rather, they see that the money set aside for appreciation is money that the manager can't show the corporate bosses as profit. The manager is investing that money into his or her employees to reinforce the idea that they are in fact the backbone of the entire operation.

As mentioned, Wegmans has made *Fortune*'s "100 Best Companies to Work For" every year since the list was created. Talk to any

Wegmans employee, and you'll hear the same gratitude and appreciation I heard when I walked through the aisles carrying a video camera. You'll find a team of men and women who are not only satisfied at their jobs but are also humbled by the opportunity to work for such a company.

It's About Doing the Right Thing

When Hurricane Sandy tore through New Jersey in October 2012, many employees at the Wegmans in the township of Ocean found themselves homeless. "They had nowhere to live," Danny Wegman told me. "We had to find ways of helping them. We had to give them a place to stay and a place to wash."

So Wegmans helped their employees find temporary housing. They even pitched in for gasoline so employees could get to and from the store. "We did that for our people so they could help our customers," Danny said. "It wasn't about the money; it was about doing the right thing."

Danny had a chance to visit the Ocean store right before he and I spoke. I could hear the emotion in his voice when he described the scene. "I was down there two weeks ago," he said. "It was one of the most emotional days I've ever had in my life, receiving thanks from our people and hearing them thank our store manager who took care of them and tried to make their lives as good as he could."

Do you think the Wegmans in Ocean, New Jersey has a retention problem? Didn't think so.

What was Wegmans' response to a disaster but a celebration of their employees and how much they mean to the company? The employees didn't "earn" the recognition by meeting some goal punched into a computer. They were simply treated like they mattered.

Of course, while loyalty and altruism are all well and good, it would be incorrect to label Wegmans' commitment to its employees as pure bleeding-heart philanthropy. Treating people like people builds trust and loyalty, which in turn builds a more solid foundation for business success. That's why Wegmans' full-time, voluntary turnover rate is at an extremely low four percent. Although the New School believes in compassion, it never loses focus on the bottom line. Talk about a win-win.

By far the best lesson to draw from the Wegmans example is the idea of continuous acknowledgement for all employees across all levels. From the moment they punch in, Wegmans employees experience a culture that has been built around acknowledging them as critically important to the company's success. There's no beginning or end to the acknowledgement. It's simply ingrained in the culture.

Breaking Free of the 10-80-10 Management Mindset

Under an Old School regime, managers focus 80 percent of their time dealing with 20 percent of their workforce—the 10 percent who comprise their top performers and the 10 percent who are their problem children. Managers know they have to keep the superstars inspired and happy, so they constantly recognize their contributions. And managers know they need to keep the misfits' noses to the grindstone, pushing them and always keeping a close eye on them. The 80 percent in the middle are generally ignored and treated as the "brick-in-the-wall" folks who can be pacified with an occasional set of steak knives.

In this type of culture, most of the recognition and rewards—and even simple forms of acknowledgement—are reserved for the superstars. Thus, when the morale of the workforce dips below acceptable levels, a game of Whack-a-Mole ensues where the manager attempts to whack it back in place with threats and knee-jerk consequences. Alternatively, they try out recognition en masse to see if that will rally the team back into action. ("Thumbs up, everyone—you're all wonderful and doing a great job!") And while either route may temporarily move the sales or productivity needle, neither tactic does anything to ensure sustainable results.

Today's employees don't react well when they're being threatened, and they can sense when they're being patronized with steak-knives praise. So while managers are focusing 80 percent of their time and energy with the superstars and the misfits, the bricks are left out of the bargain. They are, in essence, ignored. It's these employees who become disenfranchised, often phoning it in or leaving for greener pastures elsewhere because *their contributions go unacknowledged.*

Customers or Employees: Who's Really the Apple of Your Eye?

Count me among the hundreds of millions of Apple fanatics. I love their products and the way the company stands behind and services everything they sell. But as much as I rave about their products, I rave even more about the culture that's continually on display at Apple's retail stores.

On a Tuesday morning several months ago, I was at one of the Apple stores in a nearby mall awaiting my scheduled appointment with a "Genius," the official job title for Apple's trained and certified service technicians.

Suddenly, I heard a thunderous ovation break out on the floor. As I glanced around, I counted 27 blue-shirted Apple employees on the sales floor who had all turned away from their customers and were all applauding and cheering wildly. Like others in the store that day, I was more than a little curious as to what all this commotion was about when suddenly a young man emerged from a door in the back of the store. The noise grew even louder as he made his way toward the front doors of the room. Every employee stopped doing whatever they had been doing previously to approach him, shake his hand, give him a high five or a hug, and pat him on the back saying "Thanks, Kyle!"

It was a tribute fitting a true hero. I figured this guy was some kind of iconic celebrity in the Apple world, perhaps a relative of Steve Jobs or maybe the creator of the iPhone. So when the applause finally ceased, I asked a Genius, "Hey, who's that Kyle guy?"

"He's an associate of ours who has worked here for the last year. Today's his last day."

As I discovered later, everyone who works at an Apple Store gets this kind of reception on his or her first day *and* on his or her last day.

Think about that for a moment. It flies in the face of everything that has ever been taught about business. The customer is always number one, right?

Not so at the Apple Store. Employees literally turn their backs on customers to acknowledge and pay their respects to their own. This decision to stop helping customers, if only for a few minutes, has to be bad for business, right? Not according to Apple stock prices. In fact, this is the exactly the kind of counterculture behavior that sets Apple apart, creating legions of enthusiastic, flag-waving fans all over the world.

Woven deeply into the Apple culture is an unspoken credo that essentially says *our customers are very important to us, but our people will always be numero uno.*

The lesson: When you go out of your way to acknowledge and appreciate those on your frontl ine, the results will shine through on your bottom line.

Chet Cadieux, CEO of Tulsa, Oklahoma-based QuikTrip, told me he has built upon principles put into place when his father Chester, an Air Force veteran, and entrepreneur Burt Holmes cofounded the business in 1958. For example, from the first day employees join the company, QuikTrip makes sure they feel like they're part of the team. New hires at the Tulsa headquarters find a big tub of candy on their desks on their first day, as *Fortune* and others have noted, enticing coworkers to meet the newbies and welcome them to the team. That's acknowledgement from day one.

But more importantly, Chet knows what it means to personally recognize outstanding contributors. When a QuikTrip customer submits a note or email praising an employee, Chet sends that worker a handwritten thank-you note along with the message received from the customer. "I still believe in using monetary rewards, but I think that if you truly care and respect your employees, they can tell," he said.

Indeed they can. But, of course, this kind of personal acknowledgement requires a lot of time and energy, and that's why so many companies simply automate employee recognition through third-party cookie-cutter systems that operate much the same way customer loyalty cards work down at your neighborhood coffee shop. When a manager notices an employee has made an above-and-beyond contribution in sales, service, performance, etc., the manager awards the employee credits or points. Employees accumulate their points over time, and when they reach a certain level or goal they can then cash them in for incentives that match that point level in a catalogue. If your kids have ever stored up tickets from Chuck E. Cheese arcade games then shopped for the trinkets in the reward zone, then you get the idea. While these kinds of programs are a far better option than not having one at all, they don't carry the same kind of emotional currency—acknowledgement, if you will—of a personal note from the CEO of an $11.2 billion company. Remember that the first of the four Ps in Recognition 101 stands for Personal, and the third stands for Prompt. QuikTrip's method scores a bull's-eye here where the accumulated points method fails on both counts.

Channeling Empathy to Your Advantage

We started this book with a reflection back on the worst job you ever had. Recalling how it feels to be taken for granted, ignored, and perhaps even marginalized, you know the extreme importance of making absolutely certain that no one in your organization ever feels like just another brick in your wall. If you had been your own boss back in that situation, *what would you have done differently to engage yourself and ignite your passion for the job you were hired to do?*

In the Old School mindset, rising up the chain of command was like being initiated into a fraternity. You got hazed as a pledge, and now it's payback time. You made it through hell week, and so should your employees. Never mind that the employee you feel entitled to treat like a pledge didn't do anything to you. The Old School culture applauds the idea of "giving licks" out of some misguided view that doing so will build a legion of committed employees. What it actually does in today's world is the complete opposite. It disenfranchises employees and spits them out. At the very least, it often helps to build a culture filled with apathetic or even resentful employees who want to get the hell out of Dodge. Believe it or not, these kinds of cultures still exist.

But managers can't afford to lose empathy for their employees. In fact, the New School embraces empathy as a critical mindset when acknowledging workforce contributions. In this New School era, the smart manager draws upon his or her personal experiences to identify the best (and most human) ways to acknowledge achievement while simultaneously keeping their eye on the bottom line.

Managers and Employees on a First-Name Basis

When I listened to Don Fox, CEO of Firehouse Subs, talk to me about his workplace culture, the first word that sprang to mind was *empathy*. The sandwich chain with 850 restaurant locations in 43 states and Puerto Rico was named "Company of the Year" by KPMG in 2006. They've won the National Restaurant Association's Restaurant Neighbor Award for community service and earned the Number 5 ranking in the 2010 Zagat® Survey for service among large chains in the United States.[5]

It all begins with a simple credo Don shared with me. "I have great respect for hourly workers. I was one of them," he said, "and I try to never forget where I came from." Indeed, Don started work at age 16 washing dishes in an Italian restaurant, and he also put in years working for Six Flags and Burger King on his way up the ladder. Fox told me he well remembers the grueling hours spent working in demanding restaurant environments.

Which is why he's able to empathize with his current workforce, made up of franchisees. "It takes lots of hours and commitment and a supportive family" to find success as a franchisee, he said. He advises his franchisee area representatives to keep a sharp eye out for anyone who may be hitting the wall and need more acknowledgement and support.

But it goes deeper than that. A few years back, Don took his act on the road in a way very few CEOs of major franchises ever have by hosting regional crew rallies for thousands of frontline, hourly Firehouse Subs employees. Don told his story and discussed potential career paths for these young associates, igniting their passion by showing them how important they are to the brand. He and his C-level associates even paid wages to those workers while they were away from their stores. This sort of behavior is a radical departure from the Old School mentality that says front liners are unimportant worker bees who need to have their noses to the grindstone each and every minute they're on the clock. After the meetings, Don hung around to listen to his employees tell their stories and share their hopes, dreams—and, yes, their complaints and concerns. Talk to any of the Firehouse Subs employees who were at those crew rallies (there were 37 rallies in all), and you'll get an earful about how acknowledged, respected, and appreciated they felt. Want to see how such acknowledgement has impacted the service you get at the counter? Just visit a Firehouse Subs.

Don continues to pass this kind of empathy on to hourly people through the franchise owners. "It's painful to me if I meet a franchisee and can't remember their name," he said. "I want to show I have that deep commitment to them. These people have a deep commitment to us, and we have to have the same to them. I want the franchisees to know that we're in it with them for the long haul."

Does your CEO know your name? If you're the CEO, do you know the names of your managers? Do you recall the elation you experienced when someone you assumed didn't know who you were acknowledged your presence or even called you by name? That kind of acknowledgement is recognition in the most literal sense. And its practice throughout the organization builds a culture of excellence. Imagine how one of your managers, franchisees, or employees feels when you greet that person by name. They probably walk a little taller the rest of the day just knowing that someone so high up the chain cares enough

Imagine how one of your managers, franchisees, or employees feels when you greet that person by name. They probably walk a little taller the rest of the day just knowing that someone so high up the chain cares enough to remember.

to remember. And they'll probably feel more integral to the organization than if they were treated as just another nameless face in the crowd.

Small business owners and managers have few enough staff that they probably don't have to worry about remembering names (let's hope). But managers at larger firms probably could use a reminder from time to time to remember those critically important details like the names of the people who make up their workforce. Acknowledging your people doesn't take anything out of your pocket, but it's sure to work better than an expensive incentive program.

Employee Love Has Turned Stuffed Bears into a Successful Multimillion-Dollar Business

It's not often that you see a company founder sign her name with a smiling teddy bear face.

Founder and Chief Executive Bear of Build-A-Bear Workshop Maxine Clark began the Build-A-Bear enterprise in 1997 at one location and has since grown the business to 300 stores worldwide. Hers is a winning formula that can benefit any serious entrepreneur.

The company began with the simple idea that everyone should be able to make their own teddy bear, one with a heart (each bear has a satin heart within its stuffed body).

It's no coincidence, then, that her company has a heart and that her employees love working there. For starters, each worker gets 15 *Honey Days* a year, days to do with as they please. Need a spa day, feeling a little under the weather, want to help out at your child's school? No problem. Take a *Honey Day*.

It gets better. Corporate headquarters employees have flexible schedules or can choose to work from home, and compressed workweeks allow them to take every other Friday off. The company also holds weekly drawings for movie tickets and sporting events and sponsors group outings like Build-A-Bear Workshop Day at baseball games.

Build-A-Bear also rewards those willing to takes risks. Viewing mistakes as a way to grow, Clark gives a red pencil to each new employee who arrives at headquarters for training. Her goal is to encourage them to not fear failure. A Red Pencil Award is given to employees who make a mistake that evolves into a new product or better way of doing business. In addition, the company rewards employees of their best performing stores by making them part of the Breakthrough Operations Bears Committee. These employees share how they do their jobs, help store managers develop best practices, and brainstorm and launch new ideas.

And while many companies issue bonuses based on financial achievements, Build-A-Bear issues bonuses based on customer satisfaction. Customer satisfaction is tracked through telephone and online interviews and through emails received by the company, and store managers and associates receive bonuses if they hit a certain satisfaction score each month.

In growing her company, Clark is forging new paths, but she's also very much about tapping into the successful engagement practices of other companies. "If I see something when I'm checking into a hotel or renting a car that I think might work great for us, I'm all for giving it a try. Different things motivate different people. You've got to be willing to individualize your engagement," she said.

Clark has found distinctive ways to win the long-term loyalty of her employees. Inspiring on-fire engagement in the business is a sure-fire way to keep employee turnover extremely low and stimulate business growth. It turns out that mixing pleasure with business is a winning combination.

Igniters, Flamethrowers, and Burnout Extinguishers

By now you can probably appreciate why organizations need to get away from *recognition* as the operative word in the workplace when what's really needed is acknowledgement. Let's review some of the ways the companies profiled in this chapter have done just that.

1. **Do it the Wegmans way.** Wegmans tops the charts as a destination grocery store chain because it has reversed the Old School "customer is always first"

model. Industry leaders like Apple, Firehouse Subs, and Wegmans put employees first. In doing so, they gain harder-working, happier employees who then treat their customers the way they should be treated. *What can you do to improve employee acknowledgement throughout your culture?*

2. **Think back to your first job.** Remember what you wanted when you were a few rungs down the ladder? Take a moment to list three things you would have done differently if you had been your own boss:

   a. _____

   _____

   b. _____

   _____

   c. _____

   _____

3. **Practice empathy.** Even when you're removed from day-to-day happenings at work, it's important to remember where you came from. Having empathy for your employees will help you devise new, effective ways to acknowledge your workforce. For example, how might you do a better job of implementing the three items listed above in your own workplace?

4. **Create a culture of continual acknowledgement (Part I).** Effective acknowledgement isn't a one-and-done proposition. Today's employees feel a need to be noticed, appreciated, and even praised on a continual basis. Knowing that, what do you think is a reasonable metric for acknowledging people in your organization? Is this something that should be done annually,

quarterly, monthly, weekly, or daily? How can you ensure that no employee in your organization ever begins to feel like another brick in the wall?

5. **Create a culture of continual acknowledgement (Part II)**. Having trouble keeping track of who you've acknowledged recently? Make a list and keep track to ensure you've acknowledged your employees at least once a week. The list might include personal and professional milestones, workplace behaviors, deadlines, and goals—reminders that you should point out the great things your employees have done. Incorporate these items into your calendar so you have a daily reminder to acknowledge the people around you.

6. **Reinforce that culture even—especially—during the tough times**. The New School of recognition requires a change in focus. Think about how you might acknowledge your employees *even when performance levels aren't where you want them to be*. While you don't want to patronize them or praise them for doing less than their best, consider implementing a strategy that will help you focus on the positive. That way, when you need to address the negative there's a greater chance that it will be received in a spirit of openness and cooperation.

7. **Encourage everyone to be part of a culture of acknowledgement**. It's not only what management can do to recognize employees for good performance; it's what employees can do for each other. In a celebratory culture, employees know not only that they are appreciated by management but also that they are also appreciated by their peers. (Think of Wegmans' CARE program or the clap-in, clap-out culture at Apple Stores.)

8. **Don't spam your praise**. Recognition falls apart if it's not personal. Even though you probably have 500 friends on Facebook and almost that many connections on LinkedIn, how many of them could pick you out of a crowd? We're all starved for personal connections, for conversations meant for and directed exclusively to us. That goes double in the workplace. So instead of a generic "go team!" pep talk or the typical "Have a great day, everyone!" send off, do what Chet Cadieux at QuikTrip does and address your people individually. Call them out by name. Look them in the eye. Be specific as you tell them why they matter to you and how their contribution creates value for you and their organization.

9. **Individualize employee rewards**. Different things motivate different people. That's why Maxine Clark at Build-A-Bear gives employees 15 Honey Days a year, days they can use in any way they wish. In what ways does your company thank employees for their hard work? Days off? Flexible schedules? Store-wide (or office-wide or team-wide) bonuses for goals accomplished? What more could you do to make individual employees feel that they matter at your company?

10. **Honor the system you create**. Integrate that system into your culture. Make it *impossible* for someone who works for you to go an extended period of time without acknowledgement. And above all, never lose sight of the fact that employees who feel acknowledged for their contributions make a more effective workforce. It's not just the right thing to do; it's the profitable thing as well!

Notes

1.	Catherine Dunn, "2014 Best Companies All Stars," *Fortune*, January 16, 2014, http://fortune.com/2014/01/16/2014-best-companies-all -stars-fortunes-best-companies-to-work-for/.

2.	Geoff Herbert, "Wegmans Named Best Supermarket by *Consumer Reports*; Walmart One of the Worst," Syracuse.com, April 3, 2012, http://www.syracuse.com/news/index.ssf/2012/04/wegmans_best _supermarket.html.

3.	Dunn, "2014 Best Companies All Stars."

4.	Globoforce Workforce Mood Tracker, "Summer 2013 Report: Empowering Employees to Improve Employee Performance," 2013, http://www.globoforce.com/wp-content/uploads/2013/09/ Summer2013Moodtracker.pdf.

5.	Firehouse Subs, Press Release, accessed February 25, 2015, http:// www.firehousesubs.com/PressRoom.aspx.

Chapter Seven

AUTONOMY: Building an Army of Intrapreneurs

Remember the day you got your driver's license? Remember the excitement? Whether or not it was on your sixteenth birthday, you probably found yourself behind the wheel sometime during your teenage years. For many of us, it was our first real brush with freedom—the first of many links to our parents that we were more than ready to sever. What a moment it was.

If your parents were anything like mine, however, you likely had some restrictions on your newfound driving privileges. Maybe you weren't allowed to taxi around too many of your friends, or maybe you had to stick to a 20-mile radius. Maybe the license came with responsibilities, like running errands or finding a job to pay for your own gas and insurance.

Still, what were a few chores if it meant we could finally gain a little independence? Even driving to the store to pick up a gallon of milk in those early days seemed like an adventure. A driver's license was like our first passport, the golden ticket that enabled us to leave the nest.

Though we may not have realized it at the time, much of our excitement came down to one thing—trust. We weren't used to being trusted with much of anything—we were kids, after all. Then we came of age, and all of a sudden the state allowed us to operate an automobile. But the real trust? That came from our parents.

Looking back, I can understand the anxiety my parents had watching me take the car out. It's the same fear most parents feel. Certainly I've felt it as a dad. The question we had to ask ourselves was whether our children would return our trust with thoughtful, responsible action. Would they realize the tremendous responsibility that comes with driving? Would they heed our guidance and rise to the occasion?

No matter how well we think we raise our children, we can never answer these questions for certain. That's kind of what trust is all about. It's the absence of assurance. In this way, trust is a lot like faith. You can have faith in people only if you don't try to control their actions (and thus the outcome of those actions). The moment you begin to monitor their every move, out goes the faith.

So it's no surprise that many employers don't *really* trust their employees. After all, it's the employer's business, their department, their division at stake. It's their butt on the line if something goes wrong.

As you've probably figured out by now, we're going to talk a lot about trust in this chapter. That's because it's the foundational element of any healthy relationship, whether it's between spouses, friends, parents and children, or employers and employees. For the relationship to work, both sides need some independence—some autonomy—lest they suffocate from too much smothering. Children who can't break free of their parents' authority won't become healthy, fully functioning adults. The same goes for employees.

It's no surprise that many employers don't *really* trust their employees.

I Trust You About as Far as I Can Throw You

You probably want people to work for you the way you would work for you (if you were able to clone yourself, that is). Makes perfect sense. Where the problem comes in is when leaders want their employees to give their all while doing exactly what they're told—no more, no less.

In this day and age, some companies still expect employees to be humbly submissive and overly dependent on their managers' orders and oversight. The manager says jump, and the obedient employees ask "how high?" These employers demand accountability from their employees without giving an ounce of real trust in return. The way they see it, employees are like children (and unruly children at that). They must be told what to do. Watched so they don't misbehave. Halted in their tracks before they ever make a mistake. Reined in if they try to do their own thing.

Imagine that you're such an employee. You would bristle at such treatment. Or you'd quit. Maybe both.

But the Old School doesn't get that. Instead, they consider it a win if their employees meet all the bottom-scraping, bare-minimum items on their checklist.

Employee "Achievement"	What Old School Management Counts as a "Win"	WHAT THE NEW SCHOOL CALLS IT
Employees arrive to work. Their onsite presence is then monitored throughout the workday.	They actually showed up. If all goes well, they won't flee the building before the workday's over.	**Putting Butts in Chairs**
Employees take orders that flow from the top down. They mentally check out, doing what they're told to do—no more, no less.	They're moving quickly or slowly and working hard or hardly at all and ultimately doing somewhere between 0–100 percent of what's expected of them.	**Sleepwalking**

Employee "Achievement"	What Old School Management Counts as a "Win"	WHAT THE NEW SCHOOL CALLS IT
Because employees can't be trusted, they're micromanaged by those higher up on the chain to ensure they don't slack off or screw up.	They constantly need to be told what to do and how to do it. Their work requires continual oversight. (But hey, at least they're still here—in body if not in spirit.)	Babysitting
Employees stare at the clock on the wall in the hopes they can magically make the minute hand move faster. Then they beat a path for the exit the second their day is over.	They stuck around exactly as long as they were supposed to. Talk about a banner day.	Getting the Hell Out of Dodge

Do you have employees whose "achievements" resemble the ones above? Do these kinds of achievements fit your description of a banner day? At the end of that banner day, what exactly are these employees accomplishing?

Because it can sometimes seem difficult to gauge productivity, many managers feel that all they can do is make sure their employees are present and accounted for and doing…something.

Here's the thing. The more managers accept "something" as good enough, the more those managers are going to reinforce their own negative beliefs about their employees while simultaneously eroding employee trust. (ERs resent having to babysit, just as EEs resent being babysat.) But the fact of the matter remains that the ERs are forced to babysit (they themselves might say) because employees arrive late, take long lunches, slack off, don't care about what's good for the company, and take every opportunity to exploit any chink in the carefully constructed corporate armor so they can kill time and goof off. Then to top it all off, they leave early if no one's watching. The way these managers see it, they have to crack the whip in order to keep the place from becoming a freewheeling fun fest or a sea of inertia.

And yet ensuring employees are doing "something" isn't good enough. Not by a long shot. It's too nebulous, too vague. Confirming employees' onsite presence during the stipulated hours of the workday vs. evaluating their performance is nothing more than an attempt to rationalize a lack of management understanding of the tasks to be performed and the level of effort required to complete those tasks.

Before we go much further, let's point out the elephant in the room. These kinds of employees exist. In the past you have employed these types of people. You may be employing some of them now. How do you really know if the employee standing in front of you is a box checker or a superstar in the making? When you boil it down, how many people in this world do *you* really trust? I bet it's not a long list. People who trust too easily often get burned. Especially as we get older, we realize how valuable our trust is—it's a gift reserved for those who have earned it.

Nonetheless, falling back on these kinds of employee stereotypes is unproductive at best, extremely damaging at worst. Want to quit babysitting the butts-in-chairs crew? Want them to do the jobs they were hired to do instead of breaking their backs to get the hell out of Dodge? As we'll soon see, *leaders who are seeking on-fire performance from their employees need to be the ones to lead the charge. They need to show trust in order to earn trust.*

Being Smart Enough to Realize You're Not Smart Enough, and Then Hire Someone Who Is

When entrepreneur and visionary Pierre Omidyar started eBay in 1995, he intentionally created an office culture that was an extension of his personality—relaxed and very un-corporate. A few years later, he wanted to take eBay public. The problem? He had no clue how to do it.[1]

So what did he do? He hired a corporate suit in the person of Meg Whitman. Whitman was everything that eBay wasn't—an MBA-trained executive who had been employed at some of the biggest corporations in the world, including Procter & Gamble and Hasbro. In her first year as eBay's president and CEO, Whitman took the company public and made Omidyar a billionaire in the process. In her 10 years at the helm, she also oversaw eBay's expansion from a company of 30 employees with $4 million in annual revenue to a company of 15,000 employees and $8 billion.

Omidyar sealed his legacy with the founding of eBay, but he set the bar with his hiring of Whitman. By acknowledging his shortcomings and trusting Whitman to do what he could not, Omidyar took a big risk, making a fortune and creating thousands of jobs in the process.

Autonomy Means Different Things to Different People

So how do you get your people to work for you the way you would work for you? Give them some autonomy.

On-fire employees—the kind you're looking to hire and keep—are looking for some latitude to make decisions in the workplace. The best companies in the world, in turn, trust and empower these employees to think and act on their own. As it turns out, both the EEs and the ERs win.

In its 2014 Employee Satisfaction and Job Engagement survey, the Society for Human Resource Management found that 47 percent of employees feel that autonomy and independence contribute greatly to job satisfaction.[2] In response, the survey's authors write: "Even though management may establish goals and objectives for the organization, giving employees the freedom and flexibility to decide how and when they complete projects may improve employee satisfaction and engagement. Holding employees accountable for their work outcomes motivates them to produce better results."

Now, for point of clarification, we're not talking about giving employees absolute autonomy. Even if some of your employees seem to have loads of freedom because they telecommute, it doesn't mean their work lives should lack direction or structure. The truth is that many employees want to feel that they have some independence and a voice, but they don't want to go it alone. They want guidance and support along the way.

Workplace autonomy has the potential to break employers and employees out of overly constrictive parent/child patterns, though it's important to note that autonomy means different things at different organizations and to different people. What looks like workplace freedom to one person may look like total chaos to another. To some, autonomy means setting their own hours, while others may see it as the freedom to perform a task their own way—to decide what they do and how and when they do it. For example, autonomy might involve letting employees weigh in on their schedules, choose to work onsite or at home, or decide how to do their work.

On-fire employees—the kind you're looking to hire and keep—are looking for some latitude to make decisions in the workplace.

Regardless what autonomy looks like at your particular organization, taking into account the considerations described in the sections below can help to bring the on-fire results you seek.

Big Brother Is Watching

The invasive use of technology can also erode the trust between the ERs and the EEs, especially if employees feel they're being watched by Big Brother. These days, advanced software, surveillance cameras, and other sophisticated technologies enable managers to maintain workplace security or even monitor worker productivity and behaviors down to the keystroke.

In most cases, such "oversight" is done behind the employee's back but not without the employee's consent. Employment contracts often permit monitoring, email filters and email spying, GPS tracking, and other kinds of computer and phone surveillance.

A decade ago, companies were most concerned with limiting web-surfing. These companies often banned certain sites or restricted Internet access altogether. Some companies still follow this route, of course, though the practice seems to be on the decline. The simple fact is that the Internet has grown to such an extent and infiltrated so many corners of our lives that it's difficult to differentiate between legitimate work-related sites and those that aren't. And in today's bring-your-own-device (smart phone) era, it's kind of silly to expend a lot of energy blocking sites on company PCs.

And the next generation of technology threatens to make the types of surveillance described above seem almost quaint. For instance, systems like Hitachi's Business Microscope use sensor technology to analyze company communication and activities and track employee movement.[3] A spokesperson for a company that analyzes this data told the *Independent* (U.K.), "every week we figure out more things to track."

Still, it can be hard to resist such technology. We have it, so why not use it? But savvy employers need to understand all of the consequences. "Cutting-edge" capabilities sometimes enable invasion of privacy. In the same article, Nick Pickles, director of civil liberties organization Big Brother Watch, is quoted as saying, "The danger is that this technology can turn your staff into data points. As a manager there may be a clear attraction to having lots of data about how your business and your employees are working, but you may be undermining the very trust you require to maintain a conducive and happy workplace."[4]

For the most part, we've avoided discussing technology in this book. That's because however much technology changes the workplace, the pillars of an on-fire workforce never change. But here's an example of technology actually reinforcing the Old School command-and-control mentality. It's a growing trend, and a precarious one at that.

Fostering a Workforce That Can Think on Its Feet

The chances are good you're looking for employees who want to be more than servants. You're probably not one of those employers or managers who just wants to fill open employment slots with people who do *exactly* as they're told—end of discussion. So the question then becomes: How can your employees earn your trust?

Start simple. First, make sure you're not hiring someone who has a warrant out for their arrest. In this age of technology and social media, there are myriad ways to check up on potential hires.

But when the issue is trust, background checks only go so far. That's why you probably have detailed hiring practices in place that help you pick the right candidates.

So when the hiring is done and the new hire comes on board, what happens next?

That's when the training begins. A couple of hours spent on HR rules and regs. Time allotted so the new hire can complete associated paperwork. Maybe another hour on corporate ethics and security policies.

Then it's off to the races. Trial by fire is the way many new employees start their jobs.

Not so at the best companies. For instance, The Container Store ensures that all new hires receive hundreds of hours of training before they ever set foot on the sales floor. La-Z-Boy sets its employees up for success with a three-week orientation/training program. At Wegmans, employees have to learn the information about their section down to the smallest detail. At Marriott, employees are trained to do just about any job in the hotel just in case they need to fill in for someone at a moment's notice.

But training does more than simply prepare employees to handle the rigors of the job. Training also makes employees more comfortable handling key day-to-day scenarios. The best training prepares employees to react to most anything that might happen on the job. And while training can't cover every possible contingency, it can better prepare employees to deal with exceptions—events outside the norm that require employees to think on their feet. Training makes employees feel more at ease when faced with decisions, both big and small. The right training can encourage them to use their heads and think outside the box, which will strengthen your conviction that they can be trusted with more responsibility and a greater amount of autonomy.

How much training an employee needs depends on your business, but it's up to you to provide training that covers scenarios that are both within and outside the course of the daily routine. Say you're training an employee to handle the cash register. She picks up on the technology quite easily. Great! Are you now going to send her out to deal with customers? What if the technology breaks down (as you know it will)? Do your employees know how to deal with customer frustration over technology delays? Do they know what to do if the only available option is a manual credit card slider?

The best kinds of employee training enable employees to build the confidence they need to face a variety of situations without freezing up. They also let you, the manager, know that employees can take care of themselves, even under less than ideal circumstances. In the military, the phrase "the training kicks in" describes how soldiers in combat situations react in extreme situations. They are trained so well that they act on instinct. The point is this: A well-trained workforce gives the manager the freedom to build a foundation of trust.

Build a Spirit of Intrapreneurism

Say you're willing to step up to the challenge and give your employees your trust...what then? Well, the next step's a big one, but it's critical to the success of on-fire employee engagement: You foster a company-wide culture of autonomy where those employees work on behalf of your business while also working for themselves.

That's the essence of *intrapreneurism*. Take the best elements of entrepreneurism—independence, creativity, passion, and a desire to succeed—and match them with each employee's day-to-day responsibilities. Then build a workplace environment where all of those employees perform *as if it's their own company*.

> *The best kinds of employee training enable employees to build the confidence they need to face a variety of situations without freezing up.*

Of course, this idea isn't new. In fact, some businesses strive to create such an environment by making employees part owners and offering those employees stock options and profit-sharing plans. These are often smart, sensible strategies, and by no means should they be called into question. That said, it's important to note that these strategies don't necessarily encourage intrapreneurism. Employees with profit-sharing benefits might still be micromanaged as if they're just cogs in the wheel. A stake in the company's success may mean more dollars in everyone's pockets, but it doesn't necessarily change the manner in which employees are supervised or the degree to which they're given leeway to control some aspects of their work or their workday.

Regardless of whether employees are actually part owners, instilling a culture where intrapreneurism thrives is what really leads to on-fire employee performance—especially when those intrapreneurs are bolstered by a framework that constantly pushes them to strive for success while also taking the inherent risks that come with autonomy.

Easier said than done.

A culture of autonomy involves not just trust from the employer but also accountability from the employee. It's a two-way street. So let's talk accountability for a minute. Telling employees they can start working in the way that fits them best without providing any guidance or overarching goals is like giving them permission to jump out of a plane without a 'chute. Cultures that promote autonomy need employees to work toward targeted, concrete objectives—priorities and deadlines set by the company or manager.

Think of it like establishing the rules of the game before the players take the field. The employees have the opportunity to use their strategic skills and creativity to score more points, but they also recognize that they need to play within the rules to win.

The way employees go about achieving these goals is by following a process. That process might start with a company's values (the internal rules by which a company operates), and it might include project-specific guidelines as well.

For instance, Disney has a division known as "Imagineering," where staff (*imagineers*) design and develop rides and attractions for the company's many theme parks. As the name implies, these employees' jobs involve a mix of engineering and imagination.[5]

One of the creative processes for the imagineers is known as "blue sky speculation," where ideas are generated without concerns about technical or geophysical limitations. The goal is to imagine the best possible ride or attraction first, then figure out how to build it later. Just picture the creative juices this process unleashes, particularly among a group of people whose jobs are to think up new ways to thrill people. This creative process turns the engineering principle on its head. And that's the point. It's also one of the reasons why Disney is continually able to reinvent itself with each generation.

To recap, specific, targeted goals are what even the most creative, autonomous employees should be striving toward. Far too many managers fail to appreciate the importance of goal setting and of making progress toward, tracking, and achieving those goals. Instead, those managers tend to throw their hands in the air and bemoan the fact that giving employees some freedom translates into anarchy. It necessarily means there's no way to tell who's really working and who's not. To be fair, it can be challenging at times to differentiate between moderately productive and extremely productive employees.

That's why goal setting helps. Tremendously. No matter the industry, a company must always provide its workforce with something to shoot for. Then give them the chance to hit the mark.

Entrepreneurs First, Managers Second

Olam International Limited, a global agribusiness headquartered in Singapore, operates in 65 countries with more than 11,600 customers and more than 17,000 employees worldwide. Here's what Olam CEO Sunny George Verghese and Jagdish Parihar, one of the company's managing directors, had to say about how the company helps to foster an intrapreneurial culture that values autonomy.

"An essential role of leadership is to shape the future and to stake a claim in that future," said Verghese. "Then you start managing the present from that future point of view. The two indispensable factors for a successful enterprise—developing a winning strategy and making things happen—both depend on people. Developing human capital and leadership is the only way we can sustainably differentiate ourselves."

To that end, Olam provides a stock ownership program, which gives managers an equity stake in the success of the company. Currently 40 percent of the Global Assignee Talent Pool (GATP), about 750 managers, are covered under the program. The company's short-term incentive schemes reward ownership behavior, while their equity compensation scheme helps build long-term alignment and commitment.

"Ownership is a core ethos at Olam," noted Parihar. "We believe that every manager is an entrepreneur first and a manager second. For example, nearly 250 of our GATP managers have direct profit center responsibilities. From a very early stage of their careers, Olam managers are encouraged to take risks and gain experience in all aspects of running a business."

Added Verghese, "For everyone who joins Olam, we try to uncover their 'Embedded Life Passions.' If their embedded life passion is, for example, to influence people through their words and ideas, we want to leverage that and give them the opportunity to be part of the training and development team. My role as a CEO is to help others lead and to give them the confidence to do well. If I can improve that capacity to lead, that is the biggest impact and contribution I can make to the company. Even if I am very good at developing winning strategies, who will continue to develop them after my time? But if I help others lead, then I can institutionalize leadership in the company. That is when leadership migrates from a personal capability to an organizational capacity. This is my central role, building this organizational capacity to lead. Then I know this company is in safe hands, long into the future."

Olam's One Company mindset is a tacit blend of culture, talent, and processes that allows them to compete and win in the industry. This mindset ensures they're able to sustain and develop these strengths across their businesses and geographies. The One Company mindset is strengthened by such things as a four-day workshop conducted by Verghese twice a year for all new GATP hires, as well as by reward and recognition mechanisms, including a bonus pool linked to overall company profits and a company-wide One Olam Award for great cross-company initiatives.

For Olam, leadership is about setting the future direction, aligning people in that direction, and inspiring and putting your trust in those people as they work to achieve common goals and realize their full potential. "Authenticity is at the center of good leadership. People can very quickly see through a phony leader," noted Verghese. "Put your trust in them, and they will come to understand that you have their best interests at heart."

Empower Intrapreneurs to Make Decisions

While working on this book, I inadvertently found myself in the market for a new laptop long before I had planned to have to buy one. An Apple man, I arrived at the store in search of my next machine. I prefer to shop for my new hardware in person as opposed to online for two reasons. First, I like being able to try out different options. Second, and more importantly, when it comes to a sales staff that knows its business, no one beats Apple.

During this particular store visit, I spent some time with an employee who worked on the sales floor. I told him about the work I do and about how I use my machine, and he walked me through the various laptops, noting their relative strengths and weaknesses like a gambler handicapping a horse race. When I made my choice, he went to ring me up.

"I'm going to give you a discount," he told me. "Your old machine should have lasted longer, and you're an educator."

"Really?" I asked. "You can just give me a discount?"

"Sure," he responded as if it was the most ordinary thing in the world. "We're able to make decisions like that here."

Talk about employer trust. I didn't know this guy from Adam, yet he lowered my price like I was his best friend in the world. The reason he could is because he was *empowered to make decisions.* He certainly wasn't the manager. He was just another salesperson working the floor. Yet Apple trusted him enough to give him that kind of power. It was eye-opening. And, boy, did it work. It further solidified my loyalty to Apple products.

How many discounts are Apple salespeople allowed to give out every day, week, month, or year? No idea. There's surely a limit. So, assuming it's finite, then wouldn't your average salesperson abuse the system and reserve those discounts for friends and family? Instead of handing them out to complete strangers, salespeople would probably hand them out to their buddies, right?

Of course, if Apple salespeople used discounts only to dole out favors to personal acquaintances, it would undermine the whole point of having those discounts in the first place. Apple is looking to build and reinforce customer loyalty. Apple wants to make its customers feel special. Apple employees understand these objectives and are given the autonomy to honor them by offering discounts where they feel discounts are warranted. Which is exactly what this salesperson did.

Clearly, this Apple salesman was thoroughly trained, not just in the hardware and software fields but also in basic salesmanship. He never once had to ask a colleague or a manager for help in answering my questions. But being a competent salesperson and being empowered to make decisions are two very different things.

Many companies wouldn't dare give frontline staff ad-hoc decision-making power.

And yet. Managers must be willing to trust their employees and give them some decision-making authority if they ever hope to refrain from having to babysit them all day every day. If it sounds like a bit of a chicken-and-egg problem, that's because it is. How can you give your staff the autonomy to make decisions before you fully trust them?

The key is to begin with small decisions and work your way up. One classic way to go about it is to use those occasions when your employees do come to you for help as opportunities to show trust.

We're out of printing paper? Here's the number for the supply company. Can you order 50 boxes?

The new hire needs to learn the system. Why don't you spend the afternoon walking him through it?

The customer wasn't happy with the food? Next time that happens, use your judgment and decide if you should give her a discount.

You will quickly discover who's worthy of your trust (and who abuses it) as well as better identify your employees' varied character traits and talents.

Rather than micromanaging each task an employee performs, spell out what the end result should be. Set boundaries and clearly articulate expectations while giving employees the latitude to figure out how to meet those expectations. Give them the tools they need to succeed, then get out of their way—trust them to do the job they've been hired to do. In the long run, they'll feel more connected to the work they do and more invested in the outcome.

Gradually giving employees more and more autonomy also has the added benefit of preparing employees to take advantage of future growth opportunities. As Bill Marriott told me, 50 percent of his general managers started out as hourly employees. As you might guess, employee autonomy and employee growth are closely linked.

Let Go

"I have not failed. I've just found 10,000 ways that won't work." This famous quote, of course, comes from Thomas Edison, whose words apply just as well to the employees who make up your workforce. Admittedly, fostering a culture of autonomy scares a lot of leaders. You can give your employees all the training in the world and every possible resource and tool, but what if those employees still screw up? What then?

Rather than micromanaging each task an employee performs, spell out what the end result should be. Set boundaries and clearly articulate expectations while giving employees the latitude to figure out how to meet those expectations.

Well, guess what? They will screw up. How many times have you screwed up? The point isn't that someone might make a mistake, the point is whether or not the mistake was worth making. In other words, were the employees' intentions good, and did the mistake lead to lessons learned? When employees start making their own decisions, not all of those decisions will be the right ones. But nothing shuts down a culture of autonomy more quickly than a manager who comes down hard on an employee who makes a mistake. Other employees who witness or hear about the retribution will be that much less willing to take a risk in the future. The fear of punishment for screwing up will usually outweigh their desire to succeed.

Success comes from good judgment, which comes from experience, which comes from finding the courage to make decisions—both good and bad. Made a mistake? Well then, let's work together to figure out where to go from here.

Initiative Gets Employees Where They Want to Go at Western Water Works

Twelve years ago, Bruce Himes, president of Western Water Works, noticed a teenager working with a landscape crew at his house. While it wasn't unusual to see a teen doing such work, Bruce was struck by his work ethic and the fact that he seemed to be the one in charge. Bruce pointed the teen out to his wife, Jennifer. She in turn introduced herself to the youth, who impressed her right off the bat with his easy leadership style.

That teen was Danny Gamboa, age fifteen. After chatting with him, Jennifer told him to visit Western Water Works when he turned 18 if he was looking for work. Three years later, Danny left a note at the office referencing the offer.

Today, Danny is director of sales for Western. After consistently displaying the same work ethic that impressed Bruce and his wife a decade ago, Danny has become one of the company's top-performing salespeople.

Danny's rise through the ranks says a lot about Western. Western is more interested in who a person is at the core than in the skills listed on a résumé. With $65 million in annual revenue, the Chino Hills, California-based company fosters the growth of people who wield a great deal of autonomy by encouraging those people to grow their skills in-house.

"We've found we are better served and get a better end product when someone is brought up in the company," Bruce told me.

To drive results, Western focuses on on-fire employee engagement and customer satisfaction. The company has a number of strategies in place, including:

> **Employee Surveys**. In an annual anonymous survey, employees are asked questions like, "Do you feel you have the opportunity to do what you do best every day?"

> **Bottom-Line Updates**. Leaders welcome suggestions from workers on how to improve and believe that keeping workers apprised of bottom-line results delivers better performance.

> **The "Grand Guarantee."** To show that their service is head and shoulders above anyone else's, employees took the initiative to come up with the "Grand Guarantee," a program that offers customers $1,000 if Western makes a mistake in shipping, invoicing, product quality, or delivery. Employees post a sign that shows how many days they've gone without a payout. It's a source of embarrassment if the sign shows a recent infraction, and there's friendly competition among the company's six branches to show the longest time between payouts.

Because Western believes people are either intrinsically motivated or they're not, the company makes a point of identifying and investing in those who show every indication of having the drive they're seeking. Then, simply put, Western gives those employees the tools they need, gets out of their way, and lets them achieve great things.

Western Governors University: Telecommuting Done Right

On the surface, telecommuting, an increasingly popular option that enables employees to work remotely, offers employers a pretty straightforward way to institute a culture of autonomy. Between 2005 and 2012, the number of employees who telecommuted increased by 79 percent according to the American Community Survey.[6] Technology enables employees to be more independent than ever before, and with technology getting better each year this trend is sure to continue.

Well-managed remote work can bring any number of benefits. Study after study shows that telecommuting can increase employee efficiency, lower absenteeism, improve employee morale and satisfaction, reduce attrition, and slash real estate costs.

However, telecommuting comes with its own distinct set of challenges for the employer and for the employee. As anyone who has done it knows, in some ways telecommuters feel *more* chained to the desk than if they were in the office. Employees in the office are theoretically "working" whether they truly are or not (the Butts-in-Chairs folks). But when employees telecommute, they may fear being perceived as slacking off and compensate by amping up day-to-day productivity in an attempt to justify the extra freedom they've been given. The employee's manager may be a bit nervous as well ("They had better not be slacking off!") and expect the employee to always be responsive at a moment's notice. Some companies even go so far as to run software that tells the boss whether or not you're typing, and for how long.

Faced with such scrutiny, it's no wonder some employees prefer to just go in to the office rather than deal with the hassle of being "always on call." Said another way, telecommuting can be part of a culture of autonomy, but it needs to be done right. And what better example of doing telecommuting right than an online university, where professors and students interact exclusively over the Internet? Indeed, the teaching profession provides an ideal case study in how telecommuting can influence autonomy, especially given the level of independence most professors enjoy in the classroom.

Founded in 1997 by 19 U.S. governors, Western Governors University (WGU) is an online institution of higher education. As in 100 percent online. The institution was first proposed during the 1995 meeting of the Western Governors Association. The idea was simple enough, though quite visionary for its day. With the western U.S. experiencing a population spike, Mike Leavitt, then governor of Utah, proposed using the Internet to alleviate the pressure on institutions of higher learning, which were struggling to handle the growing demand with too few resources. Fast forward two decades, and WGU serves more than 50,000 students in all 50 states. In fact, in 2012 WGU awarded more master's degrees in math education than any other U.S. institution.

The school is steadily gaining in popularity, and it's getting its share of positive press as well. In 2013, *Fast Company* ranked WGU as one of the "Top 50 Most Innovative Companies" (28th), which put WGU in the same stratosphere as Apple, Amazon, and Google.[7] In 2013, WGU came in first in an annual ranking of schools by

GuideToOnlineSchools.com.[8] In 2014, *U.S. News and World Report* ranked WGU number 1 in secondary teacher education *among all schools, physical or online*.[9] You get the idea: WGU isn't just a good online school; it's a darn good school period.

Indeed, WGU's success has helped to get rid of the stigma surrounding online colleges and universities. Online universities have traditionally suffered because they couldn't successfully recreate the physical learning environment in a virtual world. In other words, virtual instruction couldn't replace in-person instruction. Without that critical professor-student interactive relationship, online schools were never going to be truly competitive with their physical counterparts.

And that's not just because students lacked direct contact with their professors. It was also because online universities had a problem attracting top-flight professors, which in turn prompted prospective students to question the kind of education they would receive. All in all, the chips seemed stacked against any online university.

WGU Is Succeeding Against All Odds…But How?

First, by finding good professors. I had the opportunity to speak with Robert "Bob" Mendenhall, who has been president of WGU since 1999. Bob was quite clear that WGU's success starts with finding the right people to be professors, or "mentors" in WGU terminology.

"It starts during the interview process," Bob said. "We are really looking for individuals who have a passion for working with students, for helping individual students achieve success. We're looking for that undercurrent of commitment to spend time with students." WGU seeks out *teaching* professors who enjoy the simple act of teaching as opposed to research professors. What WGU really wants are *personable* applicants who can engage the students across an impersonal medium, like a computer screen.

Bob also mentioned that WGU has training centers in certain areas of the country, such as in St. Louis, Austin, Phoenix, and

Indianapolis. WGU prefers to hire applicants near these centers, because once they're hired they'll spend up to three months at the centers for training. The new hires "develop a really strong camaraderie before going home to work," Bob said.

It may seem superfluous for an online institution to worry about employee fellowship. Yet WGU mentors meet frequently (if virtually), which means that they all benefit from the interpersonal relationships they develop. The faculty are divided into teams led by a program manager. The program manager gets to decide how often the team meets online. Some teams meet weekly, while others get together daily for a "huddle." The entire company also comes together once a year for a week of training, sharing, and socializing, all as a way of maintaining interpersonal connections.

"Our faculty are called mentors because their role is really to mentor students through the program," Bob said. It's an interesting word to use. A mentor might collaborate more closely with students than a traditional professor, emphasizing a one-on-one relationship with them. Such relationships are exactly what WGU is after and what it gets. "Our students are distributed all over the country, and they report higher faculty student interaction than students at brick-and-mortar universities," he said.

"We really want to reward performance, not hours," Bob said. "So it kind of goes along with working at home. You can't effectively measure exactly how many hours they are online and what they're doing. Instead, we've developed really good metrics. Our faculty are judged on the success of the students they are responsible for—student retention, graduation rates, progress, and satisfaction. As a result, we are really flexible with time. We measure and reward people for performance not for punching a clock."

In addition to course mentors, WGU also hires student mentors, who are a combination of teaching assistants, guidance counselors, advisors, and personal assistants. Each new student is assigned a student mentor, whom they keep throughout their WGU experience. Student mentors help the student with a variety of school-related needs, but their responsibilities extend beyond that. As just one example, mentors help students with time management issues and even direct them to a WGU service called WellConnect. WellConnect provides students with free counseling, some legal advice and support, and other services to help them deal with challenges that may get in the way of their studies. As Bob noted, "these student mentors stay with their students through divorce, illness, job loss, and problems with their children."

Student mentors are also measured by the success of their students, not on hours worked. It's an open-ended goal that gives student mentors great autonomy in how they choose to best serve their students. Which is not to say that WGU doesn't have mountains of data on student progress. Students are surveyed continuously, all for the purpose of ensuring that both the course mentor and student mentor are getting the job done.

But from an autonomy standpoint, WGU mentors are not subject to typical employee constraints. The various methods WGU has devised to keep the faculty acting as a team—strenuous training, regular virtual meetings, rigorous accountability standards—support rather than detract from a culture of autonomy, which at WGU is a culture of success.

Ten Ways to Cultivate a Culture of Autonomy for On-Fire Performance

Every employee who works for you will eventually arrive at a crucial intersection, if they haven't already.

At that point, you hope they turn right and buy in to your leadership and the vision and values of your company. Turning that direction means that they see a future for themselves with your organization so they'll invest themselves fully and go all-in.

Unfortunately, some will turn left and quit on you without actually quitting. They'll take on the "me against the machine" mindset and begin looking for shortcuts and ways they can do just the MDR

(Minimum Daily Requirement) that it takes to fly below the radar and avoid getting called out or fired.

Your leadership determines their direction. Here are 10 ways to encourage your people to turn right, own their job, and control their future in your organization:

1. **Share your vision.** Help employees feel part of something bigger than themselves. Communicate your mission and vision to them early and often, and ask for their continual input so that they see what you see and are committed to working toward that result.

2. **Involve employees in goal setting and planning activities.** Seek out their ideas, knowledge, and insights, and invite them to help make important decisions. At the very least, let them see your process for making difficult decisions.

3. **Explain the why.** Don't just tell someone what to do without making absolutely certain they also understand *why* that task needs to be completed and *why* you've selected that individual for the job. Give the job context in the bigger picture of your operation.

4. **Let them choose the how.** Whenever possible, let your employees decide *how* to achieve the task you've assigned. Agree upon what constitutes a successful outcome, then let them chart their own course.

5. **Delegate authority, not just work.** Give employees a leadership role in some of the meetings they attend. Leadership skills develop over time, and they require practice.

6. **Trust them before you have to.** Eventually, you'll have to trust them, but sometimes it's worth the risk to trust them before that point to make a decision or step into a role that pushed them to the limit. Your trust in them will give them confidence, and that confidence is crucial to their personal development.

7. **Encourage them to solve their own problems.** Listen to their problems but don't bark out the answer. Instead, ask probing questions that will lead them to determine the right answer. When they get it, compliment them and tell them they don't need to ask you about similar situations; you have faith in them to figure it out.

8. **Hold them accountable**. Remember that employer trust and employee autonomy is a two-way street. Holding employees accountable for their work and for meeting established goals and deadlines motivates them to achieve better results. Don't let 'em off the hook. Demand their best effort.

9. **Provide constructive feedback**. Regardless of the results, let them know how they're doing, and give them the coaching they need to improve. Although they might not always ask for it, they want and need your feedback to further develop their knowledge and skills.

10. **Acknowledge them on the spot for stepping up**. A few seconds of genuine one-on-one acknowledgement and recognition can go a long way toward reinforcing an employee's willingness to step up and stand tall. Show you appreciate their above-and-beyond commitment with a reward that matches the result. Oftentimes, the best reward is additional trust and an added level of responsibility.

Igniters, Flamethrowers, and Burnout Extinguishers

1. In what specific ways do you encourage intrapreneurship at your company? What specific things might you do to encourage greater levels of intrapreneurship in the future?

2. When was the last time you recall that an employee made a significant mistake? How did you respond? How might you have handled the situation differently, both before the mistake occurred and afterward?

3. What kind of "Grand Guarantee" does your company offer? What would you have to do to foster a culture where your employees were willing—or, better yet, demanded—to take took ownership of mistakes in such areas as shipping, invoicing, product quality, or delivery?

4. Does your company's training and mentoring program reinforce employees' creative thinking skills and help to build the foundation for a trust-based give-and-take relationship? In what ways does your training program set employees up to succeed in taking the initiative and breaking free from restrictive parent/child workplace relationships? What system do you have in place to make sure employees who exercise autonomy also ask for and receive help when they need it?

5. Western Governors University rewards performance, not hours clocked, using a system of performance evaluation metrics. What do you see as the strengths of such a system, and what are the potential pitfalls? How does your company evaluate employee performance outside of hours recorded on a timesheet or punched in a clock?

6. The next time your employees turn to you for "the" right answer, suggest that they figure it out themselves. Ask them, "What do you think?" Then stand back and watch the wheels turn. Show your team that you trust their judgment, and you may be surprised at how much suppressed energy and ambition have been lingering under the surface.

7. Giving employees some autonomy requires a smart management approach along with a clear definition of the contributions employees are expected to make and the results employees are required to achieve. It also requires great diligence in holding people accountable. What steps can you take to help ensure you create the right balance between autonomy and accountability?

8. What do you think about the Apple employee's decision to offer a discount on the spot without first

checking with management? Think about how much trust Apple management must have in its employees to allow them to use their judgment in such a manner. What would you have to do to be able to show that much trust in your employees?

9. One of the creative processes for Disney's imagineers is known as "blue sky speculation," where the goal is to imagine the best possible ride or attraction first, then figure out how to build it later. Does such freedom seem like a flight of fancy? A complete waste of time? What kinds of results might your team achieve if they had the opportunities to think outside the box?

*Don't just tell someone what to do without making absolutely certain they also understand **why** that task needs to be completed and **why** you've selected that individual for the job. Give the job context in the bigger picture of your operation.*

10. Thomas Watson Sr., Former Chairman and CEO of IBM, was once asked if he was going to fire an employee who made a mistake that cost the company $600,000. "No," he is said to have replied, "I just spent $600,000 training him. Why would I want somebody else to hire his experience?" How might you have reacted to such a costly mistake? What kinds of training, mentoring, and other preparation would you give employees before allowing them to exercise such autonomy? How would you prepare the employee to take on an important intrapreneurial role? And what would you do to ensure the employee has the resources and support needed day in and day out so that critical decisions aren't ever made in a vacuum?

Notes

1. Adam Cohen, "Going, Going, Gone: Meg Whitman Leaves eBay," The Board, *The New York Times* Opinion Pages, January 25, 2008, http://theboard.blogs.nytimes.com/2008/01/25/going -going-gone-meg-whitman-leaves-ebay/.

2. "Employee Job Satisfaction and Engagement: The Road to Economic Recovery," Society for Human Resource Management, 2014, http:// www.shrm.org/Research/SurveyFindings/Documents/14-0028 %20JobSatEngage_Report_FULL_FNL.pdf.

3. Rhodri Marsden, "Is Your Boss Spying on You?" *The Independent*, March 19, 2014, http://www.independent.co.uk/life-style/gadgets -and-tech/features/is-your-boss-spying-on-you-9203169.html.

4. Ibid.

5. Alex Wright, *The Imagineering Field Guide to the Magic Kingdom at Walt Disney World,* (New York, NY: Disney Editions, 2005).

6. Alina Tugend, "It's Clearly Undefined, but Telecommuting Is on the Rise," *The New York Times*, March 7, 2014, http://www.nytimes .com/2014/03/08/your-money/when-working-in-your-pajamas-is -more-productive.html?_r=0.

7. Anya Kamenetz, "Western Governors University, Most Innovative Companies 2013," *Fast Company*, http://www.fastcompany.com/ most-innovative-companies/2013/western-governors-university.

8. Guide to Online Schools, accessed February 26, 2015, http://www .guidetoonlineschools.com/online-colleges.

9. NCTQ, "2014 Teacher Prep Rankings," *U.S. News & World Report*, http://www.usnews.com/education/nctq?program=secondary.

Chapter Eight

COMMUNICATION:
The Inextricable Link between Transparency and Trust

You've got an early morning flight for an important business dinner with an important client. One connection to make, but all in all it's a pretty basic travel day.

You arrive to the airport on time. You go through all the hassles of clearing security and boarding the plane with your correct group. You take your assigned seat and buckle in. The plane pulls away from the gate and taxis out. Looking good. The flight attendants begin their safety routine, and you even pretend to follow along. Inwardly you smile. You did everything you were supposed to do, just as a conscientious traveler should. Nothing to do now but sit back, relax, and look over those presentation slides.

But instead of taking off, the plane screeches to a stop on the tarmac. Five minutes. Ten minutes. Fifteen. You look out the window. Bright, beautiful day, not a cloud in sight. Why aren't we airborne, you wonder. What's the holdup? The passengers around you start to grumble and speculate about the reasons for the delay.

Twenty minutes. Thirty. You open a book and attempt a page or two. No good. It's getting hot in there. Beads of sweat coat your forehead. Making your connection is looking more and more like a dream. You exchange eye rolls with your seatmates, then glare at the flight attendants in the hopes that one of them will say something. Surely someone's going to explain what's going on, right?

Then a voice from on high.

"Ladies and gentlemen, this is your captain speaking. As you may have noticed, we haven't taken off yet." (A spattering of derisive snorts erupts throughout the cabin.) "I expect we'll get departure confirmation anytime now. Until then, please remain seated with your seatbelt fastened."

That's it? That's all you've got, Captain Obvious? You're not going to give out any more information than that? In exasperation, you plug in your headphones and tune to air traffic control, trying to latch on to any bit of relevant information.

Forty-five minutes. An hour. You look up the aisle once more. The flight attendants are still seated, chatting away. Then again, they're getting paid, and they deal with delays all the time. Can't they figure out what the holdup is and share it with us?

The captain comes on again. Finally, some news! "Hey, folks, we're still waiting for clearance on this mechanical issue, and then we need to take care of the paperwork. It shouldn't be too long now. Please remain seated with your seatbelts on."

Okay, at least now we know it's a mechanical issue. But what kind? Is the plane safe to fly? Can't they begin the paperwork right now so we can leave the minute the mechanical issue is repaired?

By now, passengers are squirming in their seats and grumbling voices are rising. A baby starts to cry for the third time. A kid screams as he runs down the aisle. Part of you wants to join him.

So much for making your connecting flight. You're now hoping there's a backup flight that will get you in for this meeting, but you'll first need to stop and buy a new shirt. The one you have on is soaked in perspiration.

Poor Communication Is a Culture Killer

We all have our own stories about terrible flights with mystery delays. We should be used to such flights by now, yet we always seem to get annoyed. It's not like we, the passengers, can do anything about mechanical problems, weather delays, or whatever else is keeping the plane from taking off. So what's really bugging us? Our exasperation boils down a simple lack of information. When we don't know what's going on, we feel frustrated. Powerless. Will I miss my connecting flight? Will I be late for my meeting? What's going on, why, and when will it end?

In cultures with poor communication channels, these are the questions many employees ask themselves about their companies, their jobs, and their leaders and managers. Like passengers stuck on a grounded plane, employees get impatient when their company drips information like a leaky faucet. Unlike passengers on that plane, however, employees can get up leave. And as today's tumultuous turnover percentages reveal, many of them do.

Bad things happen to good companies, and even when employees aren't to blame and can't really do anything to right their ship, they still want to know what's going on. When management chooses not to disclose the extent of the difficulties they're facing, trust begins to erode, and the workplace culture is fractured.

Without straightforward information from the upper ranks, employees are left guessing, speculating as to what has really happened and what it means for them. Even if they don't quit, workers may begin to disengage and lose confidence in their company, feeling that their employer isn't looking out for their best interests. A bunker mentality develops as they shift into survival mode. Rumors circulate. Gossip fills the gap where accurate information should be flowing. *Will there be layoffs? Pay cuts? Organizational changes that ruin everything we like about how we work?*

Bad news works its way through a company like a virus infecting everyone it touches. Even if the actual problem being concealed isn't all that severe, a culture that attempts to keep all challenges cloaked in secrecy can find itself with much higher turnover than it should. After all, no one wants to go down with a sinking ship, and when workers feel like management is withholding troubling news, they're left to assume the very worst.

When management chooses not to disclose the extent of the difficulties they're facing, trust begins to erode, and the workplace culture is fractured.

To be clear, communication channels in an on-fire culture are always open and free flowing, not only during times of crisis. Just like airline passengers expect to hear informative updates from the cockpit at various intervals throughout a smooth, on-time flight, engagement grows when employees receive regular updates from their leaders reassuring them that their organization is on target with its goals and clear blue skies are ahead.

What to Share and When—An Employer's Prerogative

Regardless of the company or industry in question, there are three specific types of information that are controlled by management and that have to potential to flow through to employees at any level: What employees need to know, what employees should know, and what employees want to know.

1. What Employees Need to Know

Employees must have some information in order to do their jobs effectively (e.g., job training, safety precautions, mandated company rules and policies, and minimum performance expectations). In many cases, employers are legally bound to disclose this information, but even when they're not it would be extremely foolish for management to withhold from employees anything that fits in this category.

2. What Employees Should Know

Employees should have a basic working knowledge of the company that employs them. This knowledge includes the company's history, ownership structure, management hierarchy, basic product/service lines, and major competitors, as well as the company's mission, goals, core values, and competitive advantages in the marketplace.

In addition, employees should know anything that Wall Street knows about the company, as well as anything that is being reported about the company by the media. Most importantly, this information should be made available to employees before it is released to the general public.

3. What Employees Want to Know

In the employee version of a utopian universe, employees would be privy to everything their CEO knows about their company. Naturally, this is not possible—or even plausible. Nor would it be wise for any company to share all of its information with every employee. But suffice it to say, employees want to know what's really happening, not only within their industry, but also regarding all of the developments, changes, and updates that are taking place within their company—especially those that can have any impact at all on their jobs and their future.

What Employees Really Want to Know but Are Often Afraid to Ask

The Good

Just like every superstar athlete wants to play for a championship team, every employee wants to work for a winning company.

Some will even put up with a terrible job (for a time) just so that they can boast about where they work. But as most of us don't work at a household name company, we at least wish we could brag about working at a successful company. Bragging, of course, is the result of pride. Employees want to be proud of where they work.

Because pride is a huge motivator, companies would do well to give employees every reason to be proud. Make the most out of every big sale, every new client, every profitable quarter. Can your employees rattle off a dozen great things your company has done recently? If not, maybe management needs to model the level of enthusiasm it seeks from its workforce. Employees will never be more excited about great company news than you are. If you're excited, and if you communicate that excitement, then employees stand a chance of at least matching your energy and enthusiasm.

Even if only one department or division is largely responsible for the company's success, spread that success company wide (while being sure to recognize the contributions of the responsible division). Share the congratulatory wealth. For the rest of the company, it's like bragging that your favorite football team won the Super Bowl. You yourself didn't win the Super Bowl, but what red-blooded American football fan lets that get in the way of the thrill of a Super Bowl victory? So when it comes to your successes—the good—be loud and proud.

The Bad

When Mom and Dad catch their child's hand in the cookie jar, what is the child's first instinct? To cover up the "crime" and avoid judgment and punishment. Their first instinct is to lie. Some things we never grow out of, and as with people so it is with companies. Upon the receipt of bad news, the first instinct of many companies is to hide that news or to lie about it outright. Companies have a natural predilection for avoiding embarrassment, and if they can manage to deflect the heat by putting a spin on bad news or laying the blame at someone else's feet, then all the better.

However, the truth usually comes out eventually. And just like we all discovered when we were kids, our efforts to deny wrongdoing, cover it up, or blame it on someone else cost us much more in the long run than if we would have simply fessed up and faced the music in the first place.

No matter what the situation, employees feel a stronger connection to their leaders and their company when they feel they are kept accurately informed and continually updated with any and all developments (just like a passenger on a delayed flight). If they're treated like the general public and have to hear negative reports about their company as they unfold online or via the media, employees become angry and confused, and they quickly lose trust in the leaders they feel have deceived them.

No matter what the situation, employees feel a stronger connection to their leaders and their company when they feel they are kept accurately informed and continually updated with any and all developments.

Great companies are run by great leaders, but those leaders are human, and humans make mistakes. When bad decisions cause a company to go through tough times, it's critical for employees to band together, dig in, and work diligently to overcome those challenges. Such camaraderie happens smoothly and organically in cultures that are rooted in trust, openness, and transparency, but it rarely happens in cultures where employees feel they are uninformed or, worse, misinformed.

The Change

The "change" is a term applied to information about what the company is doing differently today than it did yesterday and about what it is going to do differently tomorrow. Employees want to know the direction the organization is heading, how it's meeting new challenges, and where it projects itself to be at various intervals down the road.

Some changes are good, as in new products, patents, services, and revenue streams. But even good changes bring on a degree of uncertainty and tend to raise employee anxiety levels. That's why so many companies are blanketed in secrecy and even misinformation (e.g., "This report is only for VP level and above," or "Make sure HR doesn't catch wind of this!"). In some cases, the reasons for secrecy are justified. But in many cases, they're not.

When leaders share current and future change with employees, they reinforce a culture of transparency. Rather than treating employees like cogs in a wheel, companies treat them like they have a stake in the game—which they do. Savvy employers recognize that employees deserve to know—and need to know—simply because they work at the company. They are part of the team, and it's all for one and one for all regardless of the circumstances or situation.

Communicating Through Crisis: Columbine High School

I had a chance to speak to Frank DeAngelis, the principal at Columbine High School in Littleton, Colorado, shortly before he retired in 2014. Immediately following the tragedy that rocked the world in 1999, DeAngelis vowed that he would remain Columbine's principal until the class of first grade students in the elementary schools that fed into the high school had graduated. His goal was to prevent a mass exodus of faculty and staff and restore peace and stability to a deeply wounded community.

The thing I had to stress after this crisis is that different people were in different places. I had staff who wanted to go right back in and teach algebra, some who wanted to immediately open up and talk about their experience on that day, some who didn't want to talk at all about what had happened, and a lot of teachers and staff who fell somewhere in between. I had to respect where each individual was at various times throughout the harrowing process and let them know that I supported them 100 percent regardless of how they felt.

Now, I have never been a "sit behind the desk" office principal. I've always spent at least one hour a day in the classrooms with my teachers, but after the crisis my visibility became even more important. My staff needed to see me, to read my expression, and to know that I wasn't going anywhere. I had to remind them that we are only as strong as each and every person on our staff and assure them that Columbine is an incredible school and that our best days were still to come.

Most importantly, I spoke from the heart. I can remember someone telling me that leaders who cry lose all their power. I respectfully replied that if the situation warrants my getting emotional, I'm going to be emotional, and if that type of leader can't lead this community then I guess I'm finished. I refuse to be someone I'm not. Allowing others to see my pain, my human side, didn't push people away; instead, it brought them closer. They saw in me someone who was willing to listen to varying opinions with an open mind. I didn't just make decisions and then walk away. I shared the reasons why I was making difficult decisions and enacting changes that affected them. But above all, I continued to tell them and show them that I cared about them as individuals and assured them that we would get through this.

His primary tool for accomplishing that objective? Communication.

That message worked then, and it still works today. An overwhelming percentage of the staff who were at Columbine on that horrible day stayed on for four years until the freshman class graduated in 2002. In fact, out of the 146 staff who were there 15 years ago, 39 are still on staff today. That's remarkable resilience, but then again, as DeAngelis himself said, "We are Columbine!"

Why Need-to-Know Communications Must Be Ushered Out

For obvious reasons, sensitive information is provided throughout the military on a need-to-know basis. This is also a common and understandable practice with various other government organizations. Intelligence agencies, for example, operate under strict hierarchies where the chain of command is absolute, and communication follows that chain in order to protect national interests and save lives.

One of the more famous examples of need-to-know thinking is the Manhattan Project, which developed the atomic bombs during World War II. By its conclusion in the summer of 1945, more than 100,000 people were working on the project at multiple sites and cities throughout the country. Shortly after the war ended, a story in *Life* magazine reported, "[p]robably no more than a few dozen men in the entire country knew the full meaning of the Manhattan Project, and perhaps only a thousand others even were aware that work on atoms was involved."[1] In other words, greater than 99 percent of the Manhattan Project workforce had no idea what they were even working on.

> When leaders share current and future change with employees, they reinforce a culture of transparency.

Clandestine activity was crucial on the Manhattan Project. And it worked for a time (even if Soviet spies eventually managed to steal America's atomic secrets). Clearly, one can envision numerous scenarios in today's cutthroat, high-tech business world where employees shouldn't be told about certain aspects of the business. It would be outright stupid for innovative companies to make public their proprietary formulas, technologies, recipes, processes, sources, and marketing strategies, so they'll go to great lengths to protect those secrets both externally and internally. Employees understand and accept that.

The damage to a workplace culture occurs when employees feel they are kept in the dark with the news, developments, and activities that directly affect their jobs and their futures. Old School line and staff leaders still defend this practice with outdated thinking. Why should they tell low-level admins how well the company did last quarter? After all, they shouldn't concern themselves with things that are above their pay grade. Why tell the sales managers about the new updated product line that's in development? That's only going to cause them to stop pushing the current line and go into hibernation mode waiting for the new product rollout.

The further employees are removed from developments, and direction of their company, the more disengaged they become. When treated like workers on the Manhattan Project, today's employees aren't going to feel valued and important, they're not going to bring their best efforts to the job, and they certainly aren't going to be motivated to achieve team goals.

The further employees are removed from the news, decisions, developments, and direction of their company, the more disengaged they become.

To avoid misconceptions, exasperation, and unnecessarily high rates of employee turnover, it's in a company's best interests to help employees feel invested in the company by keeping them as informed as possible. Need-to-know has to go.

Stand-Up Meetings for Stand-Up Employees

Think of the challenges involved in managing a hotel. Hotels, from the smallest to the largest, have multiple divisions—reception, concierge, maid service, kitchen, bell hop, restaurant, etc.—and each division runs like a miniature business. Cram all of these small businesses into one building, add a few hundred (or a few thousand) guests, shake vigorously, and you have one complex operation.

The only way this juggling act can work is if each division knows what the others are doing. That's why communication forms the foundation of hotel operations at Marriott. "Every morning we have departmental stand-up meetings at our hotels," Bill Marriott told me. "These meetings give managers the opportunity to fill in their staff on those important things that impact their jobs, on their responsibilities, and on what they will be focusing on that day."

During these stand-up meetings, the hotel GM and the staff work together to identify what Bill calls the "theme of the day." What needs work? Where are we slipping a little? Then it's all hands on deck to work on improving that area. "Along the way," Bill said, "the GMs ask for input as to how things are going. What do our guests need?"

The meetings always end with a simple but profound question managers ask their employees. "What tools do you need to get your work done or to do your job more effectively?"

It's this final question that allows employees to express their needs. "We want to correct the problem then and there," Bill said. "We listen to what our employees tell us. And when people feel that they've been listened to and that their needs are attended to, they are much more inclined to stay in their jobs."

Think about it. When a problem arises at a hotel, guests usually complain to the first staff member they see. At Marriott, that staff member can't say, "It's not my problem." The problem either gets fixed then and there, or staff members bring it up with their manager. If the manager can't fix it, the manager addresses the problem at the stand-up meeting. Everyone takes responsibility.

And that's just one more reason Marriott frequently appears as one of *Fortune*'s 100 Best Companies to Work For.

The Direct Connection between Organizational Transparency and Employee Happiness

A transparent company is one where information between employer and employees flows freely. As Warren Bennis and Daniel Goleman write in their book *Transparency: How Leaders Create a Culture of Candor*, "An organization's capacity to compete, solve problems, innovate, meet challenges, and achieve goals—its intelligence, if you will—varies to the degree that the information flow remains healthy."[2] In other words, transparency isn't just good for engaging your employees; it's just plain good for business.

Let's turn to a scientific study for further evidence. In 2013, HR consulting firm TINYPulse released the findings of a study that identified seven trends disrupting today's workplace. After surveying more than 300 global organizations and sifting through 40,000 responses, TINYPulse found that the number one factor contributing to employee happiness is transparency.[3]

The study's authors were a bit surprised by the results, as they readily admit:

> Our research unveils something we did not expect nor have seen backed by research in the popular press. There is a very strong relationship and correlation between an employee's self-reported happiness level...and the transparency of management. Rating of co-workers and team members, relationship with co-workers, and effectiveness of responding to feedback also correlated highly to employee happiness but transparency of management came out on top.

The data affirms that an informed employee is a happy employee. And it doesn't take a sleuth to conclude that a happy employee is more engaged, more productive, and more committed. Transparency is a key factor in on-fire performance.

Beyond Transparency: Are You Really Listening?

A culture built on effective communications does much more than merely share timely and relevant information with its employees; it goes to great lengths to listen to them and digest that feedback. Consider what Bill Marriott told me about his stand-up meetings. Not only are managers expected to discuss what employees are doing well and where they need to improve, but they are also encouraged to ask open-ended questions in order to solicit feedback from employees about what they need to do their jobs better. That's a powerful combination.

"A manager doesn't have to give their employees everything they ask for," Bill Marriott told me. "But they do have to listen to them and respond. If housekeepers ask their supervisors for more linens on the third floor, a supervisor must try very hard to accommodate that request immediately. But if they ask for something that management cannot deliver for them, the supervisor should at least tell the employees why their request can't be met or when it will be handled. Employees tend to stay in a job when they feel as if they are being listened to and valued."

When was the last time you asked your people what they needed to perform better in their jobs?

Employee surveys can be useful tools, but by themselves they're not enough to truly know what your people are thinking. There's no survey and there's no digital app in the world that can take the place of a manager finding a few moments of quiet, pulling one of her employees aside, and asking questions like, *"Hey, how are you making out around here? What kinds of dragons have you had to slay today? Do you have all the tools and resources you need? Are you seeing any challenges on the horizon that you're going to need help with? What can I do to support you?"*

And once her employees start to open up, the most important thing she can do is to shut up, listen, take notes, and then take action.

As Bill Marriott suggested, listening and responding are prerequisites to achieving on-fire employee performance.

A Communicating Culture at L'Oréal

With a background in startups, Michael Larrain knows the value of the entrepreneurial spirit, but he also knows that an entrepreneurial spirit doesn't often thrive at large companies.

Not so in his division at L'Oréal. As the president of L'Oréal's Active Cosmetics Division, Michael is committed to creating a culture of "intrapreneurialism," which means instilling the entrepreneurial spirit in all employees in order to spur innovative thinking and on-fire passion, ambition, and growth.

One program designed to encourage that entrepreneurial spirit among employees mimics the reality show *Shark Tank*, where contestants showcase their business or product before a panel of venture capitalists. Each team at L'Oréal spent eight weeks working with a coach on developing dozens of ideas that they presented to senior leaders during two days in New York. Decisions were made immediately on the viability of an idea, with one brand bringing a handful of ideas that were implemented straight away.

"It created a buzz throughout the entire division," Michael says. "It showed that enthusiasm, hard work, and entrepreneurship were recognized and acted upon. It has helped really give us a jump forward in creating the culture I want."

Michael went on to describe the importance of open communication to his division. "I want everyone to ask questions about why we're doing the things we're doing," he said. "I need people around me who have good experience and business sense, people who know how to ask the right questions so I'm able to pull the layers back and see a problem in a completely different manner."

That also means that everyone is encouraged to try out new ideas without feeling they'll be berated or judged. "Don't shoot down a creative idea that someone throws out," Michael said. "If you do, that person may never say anything again."

"I want my people to know that they're more than a number in this division," he told me. "I want an assistant to walk into my office and tell me what he or she thinks. I think it's extremely healthy for people to feel they have a voice."

Michael says that communicating is critical if such a fast-paced culture is to thrive, and he urges his managers to "communicate, communicate, communicate." To that end, he holds quarterly phone conferences to get feedback from sales representatives. Calls range from 45 minutes to 2 hours.

"I don't get to be in the field as much as I would like, but over the last two years we have developed a level of trust so that our sales representatives can share what they want," he said. "There is no agenda. It gives me a chance to see what morale is like and where we may be dropping the ball. It also keeps the managers on their toes because they know I've got a link directly to the people in the field."

Keeping communication open on a regular basis enables Michael and his managers to spot a worker who may be trying to shoulder too much and is headed toward burnout. While his workers understand there will be some long hours during critical periods, he tries to keep the anxiety from building and undermining their efforts.

"I really encourage our managers to be proactive in encouraging our people to have a balanced life," he noted. "With 86 percent of my division being female, we have a lot of working mothers, and I'm a father myself. I understand that you need to take time to recharge on a vacation and that you need to afford people some flexibility."

In addition, Michael believes in face-to-face (or mouth-to-ear) communication over e-communication. "I'm trying out what I call a 'huddle,'" he said. "I grab a group of people to meet for ten minutes. We don't even sit down. It's a way for me to quickly find out what's going on." He also encourages employees to pick up the phone more. "Rather than just send another email, I am forcing myself to get up and talk to people. And that's a good thing."

An Open-Door Policy Is Effective Only When the Door Is Truly Open

If you lined up a hundred managers and asked them how their employees are expected to approach them with a problem or concern, 99 of them would reply using some form of the cliché "my door is always open."

In theory, an open-door policy is the quickest way to facilitate a transparent culture where information flows freely between the ERs and the EEs. Unfortunately, it's also one of the most commonly abused terms in the workplace. Many managers say that their door is open, when in actuality the door to frank and honest dialogue with their subordinates is slammed shut. What these managers really mean is, *"My door is open when you want to approach me with good news or when you want me to use my authority to address a problem that can be solved or delegated in two minutes or less. But if you're here with a whale of a problem, or, God forbid, a personnel issue that's going to require significant time and attention, then please take it to HR or make an appointment with my admin."*

In most cultures, it's the employer who wields the communication saber, and it's the lowly employee who must yield to it. This structure stifles the flow of what could be important information and builds a brick wall between rank and file, from one level to another. Further, it inhibits important information from flowing upward, as employees are forced to exercise great caution in everything they say, picking and choosing each word carefully so as to not ruffle any feathers. Employees are left feeling scared and intimidated, not knowing if they can speak freely and candidly. That's why cultures that promote an open-door policy need to explain what is meant by the term and what the ground rules are for both parties in open-door communications.

Companies, and in particular employers or managers, must prove through their actions that they are truly receptive to employee input. They can start by getting rid of some bad habits.

First, stop assuming that an oft-repeated "door open" invitation satisfies your transparency quota.

Second, stop pretending that email and other forms of text-based communication are acceptable alternatives to face-to-face communication. Technology allows employers and employees to stay in nearly continuous contact during all hours of the day, for better or worse, which has allowed employees to unchain themselves from office desks and work remotely—a not-insignificant social trend. Yet technology has also allowed companies to diminish the value of in-person communications. I've known companies with a dozen people that have embraced technology to the extreme by encouraging in-office instant messaging—even when all 12 people worked in the same small office!

Granted, technology has provided a level of efficiency and speed unimaginable just a few years ago. However, to build a transparent culture in today's multitasking, fleet-footed age, you need to take the time to sit down with your people and have a real conversation.

Transparency requires conscious effort on the manager's part. Your door may be open, but your employees may still see a Berlin Wall separating management and staff.

Third, schedule fewer meetings. Seriously. Employees often become different people in meeting environments. They either try to hide as if they have nothing to say or, on the flip side, try to dominate the entire discussion. The charismatic, the erudite, and the braggers tend to dominate meetings, while the cautious and humble rarely get a word in edgewise. Moreover, meetings have a tendency to take on a life of their own, as if collaborative work can get done only around a conference table. Hold too many meetings, and they become something to "get through" before employees can go on with the rest of their day and get their actual work done.

To minimize meeting overload, it's far more helpful to conduct impromptu "huddles." At first blush, a manager might seem to be putting an employee on the spot. But the informal nature of a huddle ("Hey, Alice, you got a minute?") assumes that employees won't have to spend hours prepping a 50-slide PowerPoint. It also takes the pressure off, because employees know they aren't going to be graded on their preparedness or their presentation skills. It's just the manager and an employee or two: "Chris, give me your thoughts on…."

Transparency requires conscious effort on the manager's part. It's easy for companies to talk a big game but fail in the execution. Your door may be open, but your employees may still see a Berlin Wall separating management and staff.

To tear down that wall, be sure to walk the talk. Be available. Stick with employees through the good and the bad, and keep them in the loop. Build bridges of trust, mutual respect, and shared experience by opening your door and ushering the employees in. Stroll the floors, huddle, hold stand-up meetings, and hear what your people really think.

Transparency Rules Management-Labor Relations at WestJet

WestJet, a low-cost carrier based in Calgary, Alberta, won the Randstad Award for Canada's Most Attractive Employer in 2012. It was ranked number three in Aon Hewitt's 2012 List of the Best Employers in Canada, and it was one of Canada's Top 100 companies for 2012. Not bad for a little airline most Americans have never heard of.

I had the privilege of speaking with Gregg Saretsky, President and CEO of WestJet since 2010. My goal was to discover what his company was doing to gain such acclaim in what many see as one of the most problem-plagued industries.

Now, for the record, there are many things WestJet does right, but what struck me most was how WestJet bent over backward to ensure company transparency. To help me understand what they do and how they do it, Gregg told me about a decision the company was considering a couple of years ago. WestJet wanted to add a second aircraft type to compete in a different market, but the move would have had implications for the existing workforce. The new market sector had different compensation and benefits than the sector West-Jet had traditionally operated in, meaning that the employees who worked on this second aircraft would be paid differently.

This impending pay difference caused quite a stir at WestJet, where employees had come to appreciate the fairness with which management treated them. Adding a new airline with a different compensation structure threatened to upset that equality.

"We started to get a lot of pushback from WestJetters," Gregg explained to me. These WestJetters felt that the company was forsaking the values that had made it so successful. (It's also worth pointing out that these same WestJetters felt comfortable enough to express their concerns to management—that in itself is a great starting point for a healthy dialogue.) "We went to employees and told them we wanted to be very transparent with them," Gregg said. In response, Gregg and the rest of the management team took the employees' concerns to the board of directors.

"We told the board, 'We're still very committed to this new direction, but it won't work if we don't have the majority of WestJetters on our side,'" Gregg said. "They have to believe that this change is in the best interest of the company, because if they don't that's a big hit on our culture."

If the deal panned out, it would mean big bucks for the company. That's usually where the conversation in most C-suites ends. Not at WestJet.

Gregg and his team started holding town hall meetings with small groups of employees to explain what the changes would mean for them. "We talked to employees face to face. We had a Q&A on our site and a new blog to make sure everyone understood the 'why' behind starting this new airline. And before we went back to the board, we asked every employee to vote on it. If the employees didn't buy into it, we weren't going to do it."

The moment of truth came when the employees visited the ballot box. More than 90 percent of their workforce voted for the new airline. It was a big victory for Gregg, who had the company-wide buy-in he needed to feel confident in pursuing this new path.

What's more, Gregg treated the employees like the part-owners in the company that they are. Literally. If you'll recall, WestJet has an Employee Share Purchase Plan that allows employees to purchase up to 20 percent of their gross salary in WestJet shares that the company will then match. Gregg told me that 85 percent of employees take part in the program. It's little wonder why.

"We also have about 220 celebrations a year," Gregg continued. (Note that there are fewer than 220 workdays a year.) "We have a full-time dedicated staff that works on team care: they recognize life events, weddings, birthdays, births, etc." The celebratory atmosphere at WestJet is part of its "Culture Connections," company-wide events staged throughout the year that allow West-Jetters to know that they're valued members of the team.

The key here is that Gregg and the C-Suite want WestJetters to know that they value them as people first, employees second. With more than 200 celebrations annually, you're going to get to know your workforce and understand their lives outside the office. In turn, they're going to feel that you have their best interests at heart. By celebrating life events like birthdays and weddings, WestJet wants its employees to know that their wellbeing is central to their bottom line. Gregg and the rest of the corporate brass go out of their way to build a celebratory culture, regardless of performance.

Simply put, WestJet values their employees' lives *beyond the office*. We missed one of our quarter goals? Forget that for a moment, let's celebrate Susan's wedding. When employees believe that you know them and value them as people beyond what they contribute to your bottom line, then they are less likely to view you as a double-speaking corporate suit. As Gregg said, "The employees' DNA and the DNA of the business are absolutely in alignment."

At WestJet, transparency rules management-labor relations. As a non-union company, WestJet has to ensure that the workforce sees itself as equal partners in management's decisions. Transparency in compensation packages and other decisions helps alleviate whatever animosities might arise.

No Berlin Wall. No "need to know." Just ensure there's a free flow of information and recognize that two historically opposing sides—labor and management—together form one company. And the stronger the communication flow between them, the more trust that exists between them, and the stronger and more profitable the company.

Communications Are Loud and Clear at La-Z-Boy

Headquartered in Monroe, Michigan, furniture manufacturer and retailer La-Z-Boy employs more than 8,000 people throughout the U.S. and Canada. Here's what La-Z-Boy's Chairman Kurt Darrow had to say about communication at his thriving company.

A great workplace culture is one where employees believe in the corporate mission and feel they're part of the team charged with implementing that mission. It's one where employees feel valued, trust management, and know they can grow with the company. When employees approach their jobs with enthusiasm, their productivity ultimately leads to profitability for the entire enterprise.

Building a corporate culture is an evolutionary process, and keeping an open, ongoing dialogue is critical. For starters, people who are looking for employment with us are typically interviewed by multiple people within the organization. This practice empowers our people to have a voice in the hiring process while giving candidates a great opportunity to see if our company is the right fit for them.

I've learned that employees disengage when they feel they don't have a voice, are not appreciated, are not part of a team, lack professional development opportunities, and do not have appropriate work/life balance. They're engaged when we involve them in strategy sessions, tap into their ideas and opinions, and reward them financially when the company succeeds. Listening is essential—it is important to actually listen to employees, not just tell them things.

That's why we update our employees on our company's strategy and progress on a regular basis. We have an internal company blog, an e-newsletter, video updates, quarterly meetings with employees, biannual leadership conferences (for our top 100 executives), and workshops across the entire organization where we discuss strategy and goals. All of these avenues of communication foster a two-way dialogue.

Let me share an example. Like most companies, La-Z-Boy faced a very difficult period in late 2008 and early 2009. We weren't able to give raises, contribute to profit-sharing programs, or pay bonuses. We also had to eliminate some jobs and make other cuts. It was an extremely difficult period, but our people understood the challenges we were facing. We kept everyone updated about how we would weather the storm and where we were in the process of righting the ship.

I have been CEO of La-Z-Boy for 11 years, and over that time I have not only drawn on my experience as an employee coming up through the ranks but also learned the importance of being nimble and adaptable because things change—the operating environment can change, the macroeconomic environment can change, and executives can change. The key is to have an open mind, think outside the box, and tap into the best resources available. Every single person throughout our organization has helped to bring our company to where it is today—one that is operating from a position of strength. And I'm happy to say that everyone is sharing in our success.

Ten Tips for Maximizing Communication with Your Employees

1. **Speak up**. Openly share concerns with your people as they arise. Don't let little issues grow up to become big ones.

2. **Get to the point**. Ditch vague, indirect, long-winded treatises. Assign tasks clearly and directly, then clarify responsibility and expectations. Don't leave employees guessing. Rather than ask if an employee can get you a report, say, "I need that report by 5 P.M. tomorrow."

3. **Give employees your full attention**. It's not just your words that convey your message—it's also your tone, your body language, and the manner in which you respond to questions and concerns. Meet employees face to face. Have everyone put down the electronic devices. Look them in the eye. Listen to what they say. Pay attention to their reactions. Ensure comprehension and agreement.

   Openly share concerns with your people as they arise. Don't let little issues grow up to become big ones.

4. **Ask open-ended questions**. Before you make your point, you need to know what's really going on inside the head of the person you're talking to. So don't ask questions that they can answer with a yes or a no. Instead, try, "What is it about that project that is

causing you the greatest concern?" or "I'm not sure I understand what you mean—can you give me an example?"

5. **Give the straight scoop**. Tell employees how it is, not as you wish it was. Don't soft pedal. No tiptoeing around as if employees are children who can't handle the truth. And deliver bad news in person. No one wants to get an email telling them about layoffs. Indirect communication and misdirection will lead only to confusion, resentment, and conflict.

6. **Explain why**. Never tell employees what to do without explaining the rationale behind it. Give them an opportunity to embrace the bigger picture and understand how what you're asking of them benefits the overall mission of the company and how that mission impacts them. When they understand what you're asking and why, they'll reward you with peak performance.

7. **Ask employees what they think**. The greatest ideas for improving your business are in the minds of your people. Go out of your way to capture that intellectual property and put it to use.

8. **Keep your door wide open**. If you promote an open-door policy, let people know what that policy means and what, if any, ground rules are in place. Be accessible. Stroll the floors instead of making people come to you to be heard. Encourage the sharing of ideas and feedback. And look out for too much silence. Apathy and indifference are silent enemies.

9. **Manage individuals, not groups**. Talking to everyone at the same time often results in actually connecting with no one. Group communications are for

providing general information and praise, not for individual direction or criticism. Make authentic connections by inviting your employees (along with employees from other departments and groups) to meet up over coffee, breakfast, or lunch. Get to know your people as individuals and treat them as such.

10. **Course correct**. There are two things that don't exist in any workplace—perfect communication and the perfect communicator. That's why it's essential to always be evaluating your communication methods, modes, and techniques and working hard to improve wherever you can. Perfection in communication isn't possible, but the pursuit of it is essential.

Show Employees You're the Real Deal

Transparency builds trust and helps you create teams that are on fire. Lack of transparency leads to less optimal levels of performance. Transparency begins with a culture that celebrates collaboration and communication. Employees want to be respected by their peers and proud of their employer. They don't want to be overlooked, ignored, kept in the dark, or treated like they're insignificant.

Eliminate surprises and unknowns. Where are you headed? What's in store for the future? Employees want the truth. More than that, knowledge is power, and these days employees want—even demand—some power, some level of ownership over the work they do. Your goal? Maintain and strengthen their enthusiasm and commitment day in and day out—even during the tough times.

Igniters, Flamethrowers, and Burnout Extinguishers

Your people want to know if you're the real deal. How genuine are you? That means less communication over email and more personal, face-to-face engagement. Here are 10 ways to establish a precedent for openness and honesty at your company and with your people.

1. **Communicate with employees early and often.** How important is it to you that you keep the workforce informed on the health of the business, new business ventures, or why some decisions are made? In what ways do you communicate these kinds of information to your people?

2. **Identify the reasons why your company does and does not share information.** Think of times when you and your leadership team were less transparent with employees than you could have been. What kept you from sharing the information? What might have happened if you had shared it?

3. **Play the "what if" game.** For many people, transparency translates into a loss of power, authority, and leverage. What might happen if you were more transparent about the good, the bad, and the change at your company? Run potential scenarios regarding sharing a piece of bad news or details about an upcoming change. Play the "what if" game—what would happen if you shared news about _____?

4. **Identify what's trickling down to your front line.** Try this experiment. Walk around the front lines of your organization and talk informally to the people who are performing the entry-level jobs. When the

time is right, casually ask them, "So, what excites you most about the new things that we are doing here at ACME?" If they look totally confused or if they can't even speak accurately and intelligently about the new products and services, upgrades, awards, and other newsworthy things that are occurring throughout your organization, then your communication flow has a kink in it and it's in need of immediate repair! And those repairs can't be made simply by blasting out a mass email or ezine from the head office. Instead, focus on improving your channels of communication so that news directly reaches every level throughout your organization.

5. **Rethink your open-door policy**. Do you have an open-door policy? If so, how often do your employees take advantage of that policy? When they swing by, do they candidly share what they're thinking, or do they beat around the bush and seem to edit themselves? What can you personally do to make your open-door policy more effective?

> *Perfection in communication isn't possible, but the pursuit of it is essential.*

6. **Stand up**. How can you implement the Marriott system of quick stand-up meetings? What would the three most important criteria be for those meetings?

7. **Determine when information should and should not be shared**. Think of times when staff have been kept in the dark about bad news or big corporate changes. Which of those situations required absolute secrecy? Which could have been shared with employees earlier on? Are you running your own corporate Manhattan Project? If so, why?

8. **Feed the information loop**. Think of a time when big news or a big change at a company where you worked took you by surprise. Why do you think you were kept out of the loop? How did you feel upon learning this news on the back end?

9. **Recognize that employee satisfaction is linked to transparency**. In their 2013 survey, TINYpulse found that the number-one factor contributing to employee happiness is transparency. Does this result surprise you? Why do you think employees rank transparency so high?

10. **Create a culture of "intrapreneurialism."** What is your company doing to instill an entrepreneurial spirit in all of your employees in order to spur innovative thinking, passion, ambition, and growth? In what ways can you better encourage your people to ask questions about why your company is doing what it's doing?

Notes

1. Francis Sill Wickware, "Manhattan Project: Its Scientists Have Harnessed Nature's Basic Force," *Life*, August 20, 1945: 91.

2. William Bennis and Daniel Goleman, *Transparency: How Leaders Create a Culture of Candor* (San Francisco, CA: Jossey-Bass, 2008), 3–4.

3. TINYpulse, "7 Vital Trends Disrupting Today's Workplace: Results and Data from 2013 TINYpulse Employee Engagement Survey," 2013, https://www.tinypulse.com/resources/employee-engagement-survey-2013.

Chapter Nine

You Provide the Spark:
They Will Create the Fire

Nerds Rule at Culture Too

Compensation, alignment, atmosphere, growth, acknowledgement, autonomy, and communication. We've covered a lot of ground over the last eight chapters.

Let's round out the discussion of how to build an on-fire workplace culture by taking a guided tour through a 500-person high-tech company that's firing on all cylinders. This is a company that understands that their success is tied directly to (1) the quality of the people they attract, (2) their proficiency in getting those people to consistently perform up to and even beyond their potential, and (3) their ability to keep those people on their payroll for as long as possible. To get some critical insights into what they do and how they do it, we'll turn to the company's co-presidents, who will share stories and examples of how they hire and retain employees who are on fire at work.

A Glimpse at an Award-Winning New School Culture Built on All Seven Pillars

The employees file into the large auditorium in a good mood. They pick a spot on carpeted tiers made for lounging. It's Friday afternoon, and they're coming for their weekly company-wide get-together, complete with salty snacks and ice-cold beer from the keg—or kegs to be precise, as they always have several on tap.

One word immediately comes to mind in describing this crew—*informal*. No starched shirts and creased pants. One employee, a former Navy officer, wore a tie for about a week before giving in and ditching the thing. His daily shaving routine lasted a bit longer, perhaps a month, before he set that aside as well.

Bubbles of conversation float up from the assembly. You'd be able to follow along if you knew the more minute details of the blueprints of the Death Star, say, or if you had a working knowledge of Klingon. Don't be ashamed if neither tickles your fancy—other obsessive interests are just as welcome. But if you can ask about the weather in Klingon or know exactly how many TIE fighters are docked in the Death Star (answer: 7,000), then you might consider sending in an application.

The lights dim, and the conversation begins to die down. The presentation is about to begin. And nothing happens. The video screen is blank for 30 seconds, then a minute, then five. Technology failure. That's not so good, especially for a software development and website design company. Like "the wave" in a sports arena, grumbles travel from one side of the auditorium to the other.

Before an all-out mutiny erupts, a project manager rises from the crowd and sails to the front of the room. Quieting the throng, he delivers an impromptu speech acknowledging one of his programmers for work accomplished that week. When finished, he heads back to his seat to a big round of applause.

Another employee quickly takes the PM's spot in front of the audience. He too has a few words of acknowledgement for one of his employees. Before he's even done talking, a third employee has leaped up from her seat, ready to deliver a panegyric of peer praise. And so it goes. A line soon forms as employee after employee delivers a quick nod to colleagues for a job well done.

Twenty minutes later, the last employee in line returns to her seat. The rest of the afternoon's regularly scheduled programming begins, but it's all a bit anticlimactic after the spontaneous display of congratulatory speeches.

Welcome to The Nerdery, where a little thing like a malfunctioning video system never gets in the way of camaraderie, recognition, and a rip-roaring good time.

The Best Place in the World for Nerds to Work

Based in Minneapolis, Minnesota, The Nerdery began life a bit differently than most companies. The three founders—Mike Derheim, Mike Schmidt, and the late Luke Bucklin—didn't seek to build a company in order to make as much money as possible; instead, they sought to build a company where *they* would like to work. "Our goal was to try to build an environment that my two partners and I wanted to go to every day," Derheim said. "As we started to hire people and actually build the business, we continued to bring that idea forward. It was very natural. We built a framework where our employees could define the culture and be the ones responsible for making sure that this was a great place to work, a place people could be proud of."

> "Our goal was to try to build an environment that my two partners and I wanted to go to every day."
> —MIKE DERHEIM, CEO, The Nerdery

Founded in 2003 as Sierra Bravo, The Nerdery now has more than 500 employees in its offices in Minneapolis, Chicago, Kansas City, and Phoenix. Since that time, The Nerdery has outgrown multiple offices. This phenomenal growth led *Inc. Magazine* to name The Nerdery one of America's fastest growing businesses. In the last three years, the company has added 300 jobs alone.

Which isn't to say that it was all smooth sailing right out of the gate. Take the name, for instance. Sierra Bravo sounded more like a shoot-em-up video game than a company that designs software. More importantly, the name didn't really attract the kinds of people its founders wanted at their new company—people like themselves. "At first I had to convince programmers to come work for us," said President Tom O'Neill, who was then in charge of recruiting.

Confusion about the company name mirrored the company's rather obscure brand. The founders had succeeded in building a company where they wanted to work, but they had trouble attracting others who would want to work there. So after a few years in business, the entire team got together to revise the company's identity. This was something of a pet project for founder Luke Bucklin, who liked to spend his free hours reading book after book on workplace culture and business leadership.

However, Tom found the "vision and values" sessions with the rest of the company rather dull and pointless. "I was so skeptical of this fluffy vision crap," he said. "I didn't get it. In my head, I was way too busy to think about the fluffy stuff. Luke kept bringing these ideas to me, but none of them resonated."

After attending a number of the brainstorming sessions, one exasperated member of the team finally said, "I like working here because we all know what it's like to be programmers. We're nerds."

That basic insight stopped the team cold. "That clicked for me," said Tom. They suddenly realized that the mission of the company was still the founders' original vision—to be a company where *they* would like to work. But who were "they"? They were programmers; they were nerds.

Aha! "Programmers want to work at a place that really appreciates their work…and our founders still write code!" Tom said. Which is why the company's vision statement is so darn simple: "We will be the best place in the world for nerds to work."

"Our Nerds started calling our building The Nerdery," Tom said. "We heard 'The Nerdery' and said, 'That is who we are.'" And so The

Nerdery it became. I mean, what else would you call a company that aims to always be the best place in the world for nerds to work?

What Kinds of *Values* Resonate with Nerds?

When you walk into the Twin Cities office, one of the first things you'll notice are the company's Core Values plastered all over the place. We've seen this before (remember Enron?), but in this case the values actually guide The Nerdery's employees in almost every decision they make. The Nerdery's values answer an implied question: How do you bring hundreds of disparate, highly talented people—most of whom spend countless hours interfacing with megabits and microchips—together under a unified vision and mission?

The answer? Consistently remind them of that mission and the critical role they play. That's why no matter where you look at The Nerdery, these company values are in your sight line.

> **Be humble**. Mark Hurlburt, President of Prime Digital Academy, The Nerdery's school for software engineers, said, "It's not about meekness or hiding your light under a bushel. Quite the opposite: *The best idea wins.* If you think something should be different, it's not just your privilege to say something, it's your responsibility."

> **Win by empowering people**. Tom O'Neill started as a programmer at The Nerdery. Yet he quickly identified some areas in the company's recruiting process that needed work and asked the founders to be put in charge of finding and hiring the best talent. Even though he wasn't in the HR department, Tom was given the responsibility. "If someone wants to pick up a responsibility and has passion, we let them run with it," Tom said. Simple as that.

> **Constantly push boundaries**. Like most companies, The Nerdery has its core competencies, but it's not afraid to move outside those competencies when doing so makes good business sense. For instance, Tom explained that when Apple's iOS came out the feeling inside the company was to ignore it. "Mobile wasn't our thing," Tom said. But the sales/marketing team convinced the rest of the company that the mobile

market was going to be huge. The executives listened and acted accordingly. "We had to take a risk," said Tom. "We couldn't say 'no.'" Today, mobile apps account for 25 percent of The Nerdery's business.

> **Integrity in all circumstances**. On the company blog, John Mathiasen, VP of Operations, wrote, "You build your reputation over time by doing the right thing and being true to core values like *Integrity in All Circumstances*. We have a good reputation because it's built on the solid foundation of our integrity. But we need to be vigilant in preserving our reputation like the precious resource it truly is and know that it can be gone in an instant if we veer away from *Integrity in All Circumstances*."

> **Solve problems pragmatically**. Chris Locher, VP of Software Development, wrote on the blog: "What does The Nerdery do? ...We solve problems. This core value gets right down to the meat and potatoes of what we do, whereas our other core values are more about how we conduct ourselves.... One of the core characteristics of a problem solver is pragmatism. The ability to deal with the reality of the problems we're faced with while staying grounded in the reality required to successfully solve those problems means we design, engineer, manage, execute, and test high quality, useful solutions for our clients and ourselves."

Atmosphere and Acknowledgment Born of Shared Interests and Mutual Respect

Remember what it was like to go to college and have your security blanket stripped away? The surroundings were foreign, the people strange. Everyone and everything was new and different. Fear and excitement—and all their associated challenges—marked our first days away from the nest. We were given a chance to learn who we truly are without being tied down by who we had been.

It's this spirit that The Nerdery tries to capture for its employees. When you become a Nerd, you enter a workplace culture much as you once entered a college campus as a freshman. The opportunities are endless. It's your chance to be yourself and interact with others who might like some of the same things you like and have passion for the same things that get you out of bed each morning.

For instance, The Nerdery has at least 50 different clubs for people interested in everything from basketball to Hacky Sack to knitting. Anyone can start a club.

"As we've gotten bigger, these niche communities have helped build a campus-like atmosphere," Mark Hurlburt said. "When you look on the Internet, you see how hungry the world is for these types of niche interests. One of the things that's very powerful at The Nerdery is that we provide employees with a real-world outlet for those interests."

And as with college, there aren't any parents (or Big Brother authority figures) looking over your shoulder. At The Nerdery, no one cares if you spend some time on Facebook. There's no manager standing over you ready to write you up. No one is up in arms if you decide to cruise down the hallways on your scooter (though you should be prepared to share your toy with your colleagues).

At The Nerdery, no one cares if you spend some time on Facebook. There's no manager standing over you ready to write you up.

Indeed, toys are everywhere at The Nerdery. Particularly Nerf guns. What better way to break up the workday than to peg your buddy with a foam bullet? (Just be ready to receive returning fire.)

Mark told a quick story about fostering a workplace atmosphere geared toward self-described nerds. "On the way to a call, I passed a VP, a senior developer, and someone who worked in software solutions. I stopped and listened to them have a 15-minute discussion on whether something is a vegetable or fruit." Such a debate might seem rather dull to you, but it wasn't to the people in the conversation. As

Mark said, "The people who enjoy those kinds of conversations work here. It's not our job to tell them what the culture is. Rather, our job is to empower them to find their own niche in the community."

Aside from the Nerf wars and the sea of untucked shirts, what struck Mark most when he first became a Nerd was the sense of community he discovered. Mark had been used to dysfunctional workplaces where politics reigned. In true Nerd fashion, he describes his old workplaces like they were ripped out of an episode of *Game of Thrones*—ruthless, cheerless, and cutthroat. "Then I came to The Nerdery," he said, "and I saw three founders who clearly had a lot of admiration for each other. They were on the same page with where they wanted the company to go and how to get there."

Moreover, Mark said he felt challenged for the first time in his life by peers he respected, not just for their intellects but also for their work ethic and their commitment to growing the company and maintaining the culture. In his first six months at The Nerdery, Mark said he "learned more than in four years of college or [his] last two jobs."

This sense of purpose and enjoyment carries into the company's informal acknowledgement program—although *program* is too strong a word for it. The Friday afternoon sessions described earlier, formally called Bottlecap Talks, weren't the brainchild of some executive or one of the founders. Far from it.

They started something like this. Developer Minh Vu wanted to show a recently launched website to his fellow Nerds on a Friday afternoon. As enticement, Minh brought a case of beer and a bag of chips. Maybe it was his amazing work or maybe it was the prospect of free beer and snacks, but Minh's "Friday Fiesta" swiftly became a weekly event at The Nerdery.

In time, Minh's Friday Fiesta evolved into Bottlecap, now a time-honored weekly tradition. Bottlecap is anchored by a show-and-tell demonstration of a recent Nerdery project led by the team that sold it, designed it, built it, or launched it into the interactive world. Bottlecap is an opportunity for the Nerds to show off their work, highlight emerging technologies, and share lessons learned with colleagues and friends.

"Another big reason why I started this event was to get to know my coworkers," said Minh. "I was a newb [newbie] at the company and in a big city for the first time, so it was a great opportunity to socialize face to face and have a conversation. I think that's still a big draw to Bottlecap today—it's a place where a newb can come in and quickly learn about Nerdery culture."

At 4 P.M. each Friday, appetizers are served and kegs are tapped in the Twin Cities HQ lunchroom. Then at 4:30, Nerds file into the Nerditorium for the Bottlecap Talk, which has come to include a video montage of Nerds giving kudos to fellow Nerds for jobs well done throughout the week. (The Nerdery keeps a full-time videographer on staff.) There's also a "meet-the-newbs" video introducing incoming employees who started that week. Each week's Bottlecap is streamed at The Nerdery's other offices.

And most times the video system works just fine and everyone has a good, hearty laugh at all the inventive shout-outs. But even if the video system is down, that's no reason to stop the party.

Autonomy Means the Best Idea Wins

Much of The Nerdery's success as a workplace culture comes down to a simple strategy: *The best idea wins.* When put into action, this uncommon common sense concept empowers every employee to share new ideas without fear. As a result, programmers are raised up to the level of the C-suite (whether they like it or not). When the best idea wins, employees have the right *and* the responsibility to speak their minds.

Further driving this need to take risks is the "community of entrepreneurs," in Tom's words, that makes up The Nerdery workforce. To keep that entrepreneurial spirit alive, the company encourages employees to act as if nothing's sacred.

A prime example is The Nerdery's bonus structure. A few years ago, Chris Locher investigated why only a handful of employees took advantage of the company's bonus program. Chris discovered the program included a byzantine series of steps that in the end didn't really reward employees for working longer.

So Chris decided to it was time for a do-over, revamping the program to reward employees for working more than 40 hours per week. Enrollment jumped to from 20 to 120 people.

The program also bolstered The Nerdery's bottom line. With employees wanting to work more billable hours, The Nerdery got more done for its clients. "I pay out bigger bonuses and get positive impact on our bottom line of 2–3 percent," Chris said. When nothing is sacred, oftentimes the best idea does in fact win.

But empowerment and autonomy can't operate without structure. "We don't just say 'yes' to every idea," Tom said. "As our core value says, 'Solve problems pragmatically.' I've rejected many ideas that have crossed my desk. Because we don't have a million dollars to invest, we have to be pragmatic."

*Much of The Nerdery's success as a workplace culture comes down to a simple strategy: **The best idea wins.***

Another area where the company trusts its employees with decision-making is in its dev committees, which empower developers to lead The Nerdery through technology direction and thought leadership. These committees are each in charge of their own discipline or software, and they're the procedural body for each discipline and rely heavily on all developers to provide ideas on how to move the disciplines forward. The Nerdery values these efforts, investing nearly $1 million of billable time per year on committee projects. At The Nerdery, the best ideas win no matter where those ideas come from.

Ultimately, the foundation of any culture that encourages autonomy and independence of action is trust—and trust isn't much of a problem when you know everyone working for you is on fire at work. "The people at The Nerdery are really passionate about what they do," Mark said. "We allow people to do what they love. We encourage it even. People who are going to be good at The Nerdery are people who care a whole lot about programming."

As Mike Derheim noted, "The best ideas can come from absolutely anywhere. We believe we create an environment where those ideas bubble to the surface—good or bad. And if they're good, we're going to push them forward."

The Power of the (Co-)Presidency

In October 2013, Nerdery cofounder Mike Derheim gave a TEDx Talk. The subject? "What if everybody in your company was a co-president?" During Mike's engaging talk, he outlines the philosophy behind The Nerdery's practice of naming every employee a "co-president" from their very first day. In short, it's all about on-fire engagement.

"I think we have forgotten how to engage our workforce," Mike begins. "Human nature has not changed all that much in the last 100 years or so." But employees have. Mike imagines asking an imaginary grandfather what's wrong with today's emerging workforce, and he says you're likely to hear a lot of talk about "walking uphill both ways" and the debilitating sense of "entitlement" that limits today's younger employees from giving it their all. (I'm pretty sure Mike's "imaginary" grandfather was really my dad...but I digress.)

Mike rejects that type of thinking. "It can't be true," he says outright. For evidence, he points to the company he founded and continues to lead: "Engaged young people are the absolute life of The Nerdery," and he credits The Nerdery's success to the idea that everybody is a co-president.

Now, to be clear, this co-presidency isn't some corporate gimmick intended to prop up the fragile egos of frontline workers. The fact is that The Nerdery is serious. Mike expects his co-presidents to act like co-presidents. They need to invest in the company that's investing in them.

"The president is the most engaged employee in the business," Mike says in the TEDx Talk. "They care about the business because everybody is counting on them." What's more, being treated like a real co-president "gives [employees] a purpose instead of rules and policies."

In practice, this policy means that Mike's employees often step up and solve problems before he even knows they exist. The Nerdery's "success is a reflection on them," he says.

Nonetheless, this "co-president" ethos requires responsibility to work effectively. As Mike told me, "We hold everyone accountable from the management team on down—everyone is treated as co-president. Not just in power; it's the general attitude that everyone has toward each other, the amount of respect everyone feels for their coworkers. We talk about both sides of the co-presidency— the amount of responsibility that you have in that role and how we expect you to react to other people who are exercising those privileges as well. We treat each other as equals. There is no superiority."

Of course, the freedom to act as a co-president also includes the freedom to screw up. A company can't encourage the former without condoning the latter. "People are going to make horrifying mistakes," Chris Locher said. "It's okay if people fail, but they have to ask for help or at least know when to say they made a mistake. No one gets in trouble for making a mistake—only when they make a mistake and lie about it."

In his TEDx talk, Mike mentions the legendary emails his late friend and cofounder Luke Bucklin sent to everyone at the company. Always full of inspiring words and nuggets of wisdom, Luke's emails served as reminders for each and every Nerd as to why they were there. Shortly before he died, Luke sent out an email that Mike quotes in his talk:

"I remember a day when there were no managers, no directors, no coordinators, and no specialists. We only had presidents. Well, maybe one president and a couple co-presidents. Forget about your titles. Put your business card on the desk in front of you. Look at it. I'm here to tell you that this is not your title. This card does not define you. You are a co-president. You are bigger than your defined role, and you are much more than your job title. Play your part. Transcend your job title, be a hero."

An Interview with Cofounder and CIO Mike Schmidt

Having been present at the company's creation, what were the biggest challenges in building a company where you would want to work, particularly one that boasts of "Integrity in All Circumstances"?

The biggest challenge is guarding against temptations that push us away from integrity. There's constant pressure to nudge integrity from the forefront of one's decision-making process. No matter the state of the business, these forces exist. During the good times, you have to guard against hubris. During tougher times, you have to guard against fear. Often decisions made outside of integrity can lead to short-term gains but seem to never really pay off in the long run. My advice would be to understand the motivations for the decisions you make and ask if those decisions are aligned with doing the right thing.

If you were to talk to a young entrepreneur who shares the same dreams as you and your cofounders, what would be your first piece of advice?

Having good partners means everything. Mike [Derheim], Luke and I didn't always agree on everything, but we always were aligned on our core values well before we called them out as core values. We had mutual respect for and absolute trust in each other. That trust and respect allowed us to be able to lean on one another when things got tough. We made better decisions because of it.

If you were asked by a president, CEO, or founder of a long-estab-lished company what he or she could do to change their culture for the better, what would you suggest?

I would encourage them to let go. The best thing we did is we did nothing. We got out of the way. We let our culture happen. We said it's okay—more than okay—to be yourself. Bring us your ideas, and we'll try really hard to say yes. Like Bottlecap. Hell yes to Bot-tlecap even though it costs us a lot of money, well beyond just the beer and food budget. There's also the time of hundreds of people who could otherwise be doing billable client work. But it's totally worth it for us as a company to shut down early every Friday. The people and culture are just as important to a healthy company as the bottom line.

What were some of your challenges in attracting a stellar workforce when you couldn't go above and beyond by way of compensation?

Daniel Pink's book *Drive* nails it in terms of what really motivates people—autonomy, mastery, and purpose. That was essentially our playbook before we ever read the book. We set out to do something different and let people shape just what that was for themselves. Our main strategy revolves around our vision for the company—to be the best place on earth for Nerds to work.

Alternatively, did you in the early years or do you now do anything out of the ordinary when it comes to compensation—primarily as it relates to engaging your workforce?

In the beginning, we employed different strategies, most of which produced only short-term gains and proved ineffective over a lon-ger period of time. One was a bonus we paid our developers based on the efficiency of the department. It worked initially until the team grew to a point where individuals didn't feel like they could impact the results. At that point people stopped caring. All of our compensation plans failed until our current plan of empowering Nerds to earn more by working more than 40 hours per week—it's a straightforward win-win proposition. We were built by a work ethic of "whatever it takes," and in the beginning that meant some very long workweeks. Now, there's extra incentive here for that.

On a routine day, in what ways do your responsibilities intersect with maintaining or bolstering The Nerdery's culture?

> Aside from setting the stage early on in the company's history, I'm a firm believer that a strong culture has to be organic. Beyond hiring good people and setting the values of the company, I can't take much if any credit for our culture. It was created by and belongs to our employees.

COMMUNICATION and COMPENSATION at a Company of, by, and for Employees

There's a theme running through much of The Nerdery's workplace culture, one that isn't directly mentioned in The Nerdery's mission or values. It's respect. At The Nerdery, people are treated as human beings, not as a "workforce," not as "labor," not even as "employees" per se. They're treated like people, and the place they work is the place for them. It was built for them, and, boy, did they come.

When you hear the phrases *be yourself, have fun,* and *have passion,* you hear respect for the individual.

When you hear the phrase *the best idea wins,* you hear respect for the individual.

When you hear the phrase *everyone is a co-president,* you hear respect for the individual.

And Nerdery respect doesn't just begin and end with its people. The Nerdery even shows respect for applicants it doesn't hire. Chris told me that The Nerdery has a 24-hour response time for job applicants. How many of us have waited to hear back from an interview, spending anguishing days wondering whether or not we were in contention? Letting candidates know exactly where they stand is yet another way the company shows integrity.

The best thing we did is we did nothing. We got out of the way. We let our culture happen.
—MIKE SCHMIDT, CIO, *The Nerdery*

The Nerdery also doesn't reinvent the wheel with its compensation structure. The salaries offered are competitive but not the highest in the industry. That The Nerdery is able to go toe to toe with the big boys to hire top-flight talent reinforces the fact that compensation is merely the foundation of employee engagement. These days, a company needs something more to inspire on-fire employee performance. No company can win on compensation alone.

To ensure that the company listens to the needs and opinions of its people, The Nerdery runs an internal message board called "The Buzz" so employees can post thoughts, ideas, and feedback for the entire company to read. At The Nerdery, transparency is key. Chris reads The Buzz regularly to keep up with what employees are thinking. But that's not all he does.

Chris regularly strolls through the entire building, down the hallways, past cubicles, to talk with the rest of the team. He also wears a pedometer just to see how far he walks each day (it usually ranges from five to seven miles). Now The Nerdery has a fairly big office building, but to log that many miles in a single day is a feat to be admired.

"I try to learn everyone's names," Chris said. He also tries to be as approachable as possible. It seems to work too. "I have probably 100 conversations a day," he said.

This face-to-face routine didn't start on day one. "I began by just sending out a company-wide email once a week," he recalls. "But then I was told by five people in a row that they hadn't read it. So I asked ten people. Only one had read it. When I asked if there was a better way to get the pulse of the company, I was told: Just talk to us. So I do."

Growth in the Culture Garden

Not surprisingly, The Nerdery is an engine for employee growth and opportunities. "We have an imperative around growth that we want to continue to expand," Mark Hurlburt said. Tom

O'Neill's just one example. He started as a programmer during the company's earliest days and is now the company president.

To be hired, applicants must pass a Nerd Assessment Test. "When someone doesn't pass, we spend some time with the individual and recommend courses and books for them to study," said Mark Malmberg, Communications Director.

Once hired, a programmer also must pass a coding test to advance to the next level. "It's not uncommon to take the code challenge a number of times. Some top developers had to take it several times," Mark Hurlburt said.

In other words, The Nerdery isn't looking to weed people out. It's looking for the best Nerds on the planet to bring in. An applicant who shows promise is given the chance to succeed. A programmer who's part of the company is given a chance to grow. At every step of their journey, employees at The Nerdery aren't alone because they're treated with respect. And if and when an employee struggles, The Nerdery is on hand to help to help them hit challenges head-on and become the best versions of themselves they can be.

"Culture is like a garden," said Tom O'Neill. "You can plant the flowers you want and nurture the garden. But it grows organically. You can't install culture. You have to let it evolve over time. Sometimes weeds will crop up, but if your team sees the garden as their own, then they'll help get rid of them. By planting a garden, you're assuming a level of surprise—you can't manage everything. Sometimes weeds will grow, but sometimes a plant will attract butterflies, adding to the beauty of the garden."

> The Nerdery isn't looking to weed people out. It's looking for the best Nerds on the planet to bring in.

Tom's analogy summarizes another unspoken theme that permeates The Nerdery: Let it happen. The Nerdery's employees make the culture. The idea for Bottlecap came from a programmer, not from the C-suite. No one mandated that The Nerdery have 50 different clubs—that's simply a reflection of the employees' varied interests. Walking several miles a day through the corridors talking to employees isn't part of Chris's job—it's just something he does that makes him better at his job.

The workplace culture at The Nerdery wasn't part of the initial design; instead, this culture was cultivated over time. The employees all contributed to building the company. And they did so because they believed Mike Derheim, Mike Schmidt, and Luke Bucklin when they said The Nerdery would be the best possible place for nerds to work. The founders gave them the garden, but the employees planted the seeds.

These employees are on fire because their employer has consciously chosen to honor the seven pillars of workplace culture and has encouraged and rewarded them for making The Nerdery their own. Let's recap how The Nerdery did it:

- Competitive pay within reasonable limits. (**Compensation** is merely the baseline from which on-fire performance begins, all the more so at companies without a Google-sized budget.)

- Employees who are in sync with the company's mission and strive to make day-to-day decisions that are in **Alignment** with the company's core values (and those values are always in plain sight).

- A workplace **Atmosphere** that looks and feels like the employees themselves developed it over time, one that gives those employees a real-world outlet for their varied interests and keeps them looking forward to coming to work.

- A place that seeks to give some of the best employees on the planet every possible chance to achieve career

Growth (the kind of place where a programmer can one day become the company president).

🔥 An environment where praise is paramount and where employees get plenty of **Acknowledgement** for a job well done from their peers as well as their leaders.

🔥 A community of empowered, entrepreneurial co-presidents who value **Autonomy** and the jaw-dropping business and technology innovations that result when the best idea is valued above all else.

🔥 Face-to-face **Communication** and the flow of information throughout the entire organization, providing employees with a voice, and the continuous, open sharing of ideas—all to ensure everyone has a say in the direction of the organization.

Building a great culture means saying goodbye to the Old School mindset. No more Steak Knives. No more forgotten majority. No more masses of employees who kill time on your dime, eyes on the clock. No more fixation on a handful of superstars and bottom feeders while ignoring the bulk of your employees who, together, form the heartbeat of your company.

Employee disengagement may be toxic, but employee engagement isn't the antidote—it's just the starting point. That's the essence of the New Deal we introduced in the book's opening chapter: Be a better ER, and you'll be rewarded with better EEs.

Employee disengagement may be toxic, but employee engagement isn't the antidote—it's just the starting point.

When you go beyond what your workers expect, you'll build a workforce that will surprise you in ways you didn't think were possible. You'll find that they increasingly display a positive attitude, reliability, professionalism, initiative, respect, integrity, and gratitude—the seven core attributes ERs seek.

Live the seven pillars day in and day out—*compensation, alignment, atmosphere, growth, acknowledgement, autonomy, and communication*—and you'll go further than that. You'll build a workforce that will come alive with passion and performance, EEs who strive as hard for the success of your business as you do. You'll create not an engaged workforce, but a legion of loyal EEs who are *on fire.*

Index

About Eric Chester

Since 1998, Eric Chester has been the leading voice in recruiting, training, managing, motivating, and retaining the emerging workforce.

As an in-the-trenches workplace researcher and thought leader, Chester knows what it takes to attract today's enigmatic talent and get them to perform at their best. *On Fire at Work* is his fifth leadership book. His previous release, *Reviving Work Ethic: A Leader's Guide to Ending Entitlement and Restoring Pride in the Workforce* (Greenleaf, 2012) is the first business book on work ethic since 1904. He is the Founder of The Center for Work Ethic Development and created a work ethic training curriculum that is being taught at hundreds of schools, colleges, workforce centers, and organizations all over the world.

Eric Chester has delivered more than 2,000 paid speeches on three continents and is a 2004 inductee into the National Speakers Association's acclaimed CPAE Professional Speakers Hall of Fame. His clients include Harley Davidson, McDonald's, AT&T, Toys R Us, Hormel, and Wells Fargo, to name a few.

To schedule Eric for a keynote presentation,
call Christie Michelle at 303-239-9999.
OnFireAtWork.com